READERS PRAISE

This extraordinary book is a deep validation of what I have witnessed over my 40 years as a hospice worker. As this compelling book describes, there *are* indeed other planes of knowing that can become a powerful part of growing through grieving. *–Kathleen Horsdal, Hospice Worker*

Dance On! **will be a marvellous addition to those grieving.** Chidakash's warm and inviting writing style drew me to reflect on my own life and how I can evolve my relationship with my late husband and other loved ones, both on earth and in spirit. *Dance On! is* for everyone who is curious and open to discovering rich new ways to connect and be with their loved ones who have passed on. *–Anna Haltrecht, Death Cafe host*

Chidakash has opened his heart. His reflections and wisdom gained through grief are shared with the kind of strength only vulnerability can bring. *Dance On!* encourages your own awakening with stories of Shera's continued aliveness, and her expressions of love for him from her new home in spirit. I am certain she is more in love with him than ever before. *–Debra Doerksen, Spiritual Medium, Author, Workshop Facilitator*

This inspiring narrative follows the journey of a woman who embraces her final moments on her own terms, in her own home, surrounded by cherished loved ones. *Dance On! Love Beyond Grief* beautifully encapsulates the aspirations of End of Life Doulas, portraying one person's ideal transition to death. *–Jennifer Brooker, Vice President—End of Life Doula Association of Canada*

The first time I read the book I just cried. To ease someone's passing, is a great honour. But what happens after they're gone? *Dance On!* opens up a new toolbox of tangible and wholesome methods to enable each person affected by someone's passing to individually cope, in a most hopeful and healthy way. *–Laura Hughes McGrath, Frontline Care Giver*

It touches me beyond the mind. I was brought to warm nourishing tears immediately. The flow is tangible love. It is a transmission to my heart. - *Julie Howard, Personal Health Coach*

This is a powerful book with an inspiring story filled with hope for others who have suffered a huge loss of a loved one. Also, getting people to question their beliefs and look at things through different lenses is such a great and needed piece of advice in all areas. And now I'm crying again! I was blown away. *–Valerie Costa, Editor-in-Chief*

An amazingly powerful message. It certainly gave me things to mull over. There were times I had tears running down my cheeks. Times when I thought there were messages for me. Thanks for giving me other avenues to consider, other ways to hold these emotions. I loved it.
–Vickie Jensen, Author and Marine Historian

A tale of love as well as a manual on how to create it. To have a loving partner to walk through life with is one of the greatest gifts afforded a person. An equally wonderful gift is when that bond remains unbroken even in death. *–Austin Metze, Artist, Poet, Author*

This story transforms the art of life into a work of art about love that passes the boundaries of life itself. The humble honest tone carried me through a kind of cathartic healing. As I read of Shera's last days, I re-experienced the death, funeral and cremation of my first wife simultaneously. *Dance On!* will help any human who grieves.
–Robert Arne, Certified Financial Planner

Very insightful. Very, very educational. I'd catch my brain rushing off in directions I never had occasion or interest in exploring before. I found myself going back again and again to make sure I hadn't missed anything. The focus on Shera's passing is exquisite to read because of this fantastic, special relationship. *–Edward Jordan, Vice President, Unisys (ret.)*

Dance On!

LOVE

BEYOND

GRIEF

Chidakash Jordan
with Shera Street

ISBN (paperback): 978-0-9681340-4-7
ISBN (ebook): 978-0-9681340-5-4

Book design and production by www.AuthorSuccess.com

Printed in the United States of America

Cover Art *Lovers* from acrylic painting by Shera Street

Dedication

To my beloved Shera, wherever you are.

To families and loved ones who have been left behind for a while.

To those Souls that have forged their way through the lessons and challenges of this three dimensional world on their way home to the Light.

Contents

Preface

Death may come over time, sending messages ahead as reminders of our mortality. They could come in the form of health issues long before it appears on the horizon, or it may arrive on our doorstep without warning.

In my case, with Shera, my beloved partner of thirty-four years, it arrived over time. There had been many "reminders," and in her last months I had become her caregiver. As she became less and less able, I took over even her most intimate care. This had made it possible for her to stay at home until the end.

In the late afternoon of Shera's last day, in May of 2020, when it was clear that her departure was imminent, I reassured her one final time that she was safe and on her way. And then she was gone.

I had not given much thought in those last months to what would come next. I'd been totally absorbed on managing the space, caring for her, comforting her and holding on to the possibility that she would recover. By the time she left, it was enough to know that finally she did not have to endure the continuing indignities of a body that could no longer express her passions or ultimately do anything at all.

In that final week, as she lay with eyes closed, I had asked her to send me a sign now and then, to let me know how she was doing.

I could never have imagined all that would happen.

Her signs and messages came so beautifully, consistently and even playfully in the days and weeks that followed, I came to the unexpected realization that even though she may have left, Shera was not "gone." Although Shera and I had indeed embarked on our individual journeys to futures we could not know, we would continue to be "together" from time to time, loving each other.

As time progressed I was so captivated by the extraordinary unfolding of events, I found myself on a quest to understand how it could all be possible. This quest led me to realize others experiencing grief could also connect with a departed loved one in a new relationship.

The second half of this book shares what I learned about how that was possible

❖   ❖   ❖

The book offers different ways to view this story—different "lenses."

LENS I — offers a glimpse into the relationship Shera and I had, and the unfolding confusion and emotion at the moment of her passing. This lens reflects and honours the emotion and disorientation others may experience in witnessing the passing of a loved one.

LENS II — Focusses on the remarkable events, signs, and messages that started coming in the initial days after Shera's passing, and showed me she was not so far away, that love does not die, and that our relationship was continuing on.

LENS III — Looks into what I found in my "quest" to understand what had made this ongoing connection with Shera possible.

LENS IV — Illuminates ways in which others who want to recognize and receive signs and messages can continue in a new and meaningful relationship with loved ones who have gone ahead.

LENS V — Reveals how the beliefs we hold shape our perceptions, and shows how those which obstruct connection can be changed.

◆ ◆ ◆

❖ I have put diamonds at times, in the margins of chapters in Lens 1 and Lens 2, as an invitation to the reader to step back momentarily from the unfolding story and shift their focus from reading to reflection. I believe something in the associated lines may offer an insight that might be of value if they are in a similar situation.

◆ ◆ ◆

Introduction

Many of us wear glasses to help us see clearly. If we were to change the lenses we would change both what *we are able to see and* how *we see it.*

Imagine:

How differently would we "see" death if, for example, we "changed lenses" by referring to the "newly departed" as the "newly arrived"?

How differently would we experience grief if, instead of "losing loved ones" we spoke of "sending them off"?

❖ ❖ ❖

In our lives, at some time, each of us will look into the face of Death at some time, and experience grief. This thought alone, gives rise to feelings of dread in many of us. If we want to shift this dread we must look into, and beyond, what we have come to understand about death and the expectations we have of grief.

In spite of our diversity, most of us, when considering such things, have been looking through the same pair of "glasses." It is no wonder so many of us hold an expectation that at the time of a death, loss and grief are the entire picture. It may be argued however, that they are just a part of a bigger puzzle.

When we are dealing with the death or impending departure of a loved one, most of us are left to work our way through this experience on our own, carrying questions without answers and with few people to ask. It is as though each of us is going *separately* down the *same* crowded path—unaware that alternative paths are available. Paths that might soften the pain and sense of loss.

That is what this book addresses: if we are going to find a more positive alternative, we need those who have been there to show us the way. It's time to change our lenses.

The perspectives offered here are the result of my personal quest to understand the extraordinary, on-going connection I have had with my life partner since she passed on in May 2020. Once others who have had similar positive experiences join me in readily sharing them, the negative relationship our society has with death—the fear and apprehension—will gradually shift. The general view of death will become much more balanced—even life-affirming.

For anyone who has lost a loved one, going through grief at some level, and the pain that comes with it, is a fundamental part of the healing process. However, viewing the ultimate transition of death through the different lenses offered in this book will reveal ways to soften the experience of grief and open the possibility of a relationship continuing after a loved one has passed on.

◆　◆　◆

I believe at some time, all who grieve the loss of a loved one have to reconcile the persistent desire for their newly departed loved one to be with them still—a feeling, with knowing at the same time that, if they are to move on with living life, they must accept the reality of their loss.

This is reasonable of course, and it's what we've come to expect. Yet as rational and inevitable as it may be, *knowing* has never been able to fully suppress *feeling*. Emotion persists even under the pressure of Reason.

This means that even as we come to accept our loved ones are "gone," the desire in us to have them with us still continues. It simply takes a new form: we want to know how they are doing. We can't have them with us, so we wonder *where* they have gone. Many of us yearn for contact and want to receive a message from them or a sign of some kind.

So it is only natural, even as we come to accept our loved ones are "gone," that the desire continues in us to have them with us still. It simply takes a new form: we want to know how they are doing. We can't have them with us, so we wonder *where* they have gone. Many of us yearn for contact and want to receive a message from them or a sign of some kind.

This was certainly true for me with my life partner of over three decades. In the last week before she passed I asked her to send me an eagle or a heart or something, to let me know she was okay.

It was a wishful request from a place of fear as much as from love. I had to accept she was leaving and yet I was asking her for messages! At the time, I doubt that I felt such a thing was possible. I had always believed—even *if* such a thing were possible—I would need the services of a medium if I was to receive any messages. I was wrong.

From the day Shera departed, I began receiving them—signs and messages. Some of them were witnessed, and remarkably, many even came *in writing!* Events began to happen right after she left which have dramatically altered the course of my life. Changes continue to this day, as I write this, almost three years later. I am grateful so many have been witnessed by other people.

They completely transformed the feeling of loss I had at the time, in a way that dispelled my grief entirely. This effectively changed the "glasses" through which I had been seeing things, and made me realize that Shera had not "left," and that we were continuing in a new kind of relationship.

These new lenses opened up a new world to me in ways I could not have imagined, and certainly could never have hoped for. They put me on a quest to understand what had made it possible? How could experiencing the loss of my life partner lead me to feeling I have been so blessed?

The second half of this book is dedicated to sharing the insights I gained on how these ongoing connections could also be possible for others who have similarly suffered loss.

Loving relationships can continue.

◆　◆　◆

Over the years since Shera's passing, I have discovered through recounting my stories, that ongoing connections after death are certainly not unique to me. Many people have responded with comparable stories of their own.

Why do we hear so little about such things in our day-to-day conversations? I believe such stories are often left untold because they lie outside a kind of unwritten social consensus of what is "normal" and what are considered to be acceptable topics. Yet such stories need to be told so those who would benefit from them have a chance to hear them.

Of course, following a death, understandably, survivors may desire privacy. However, it is more likely a generally held fear of death that leads people to avoid the topic in conversation. It gives rise to a feeling of discomfort. The result of this is a subtle, mutually sustained taboo on the subject: "You don't talk about it, and I won't ask."

However, it is the Unknown itself which is one of the major triggers of fear and which often leads to avoidance. Unfortunately, this doesn't serve us in the long run. I know in my case, when I felt lost and confused at the time of Shera's passing, I would have loved to have had some kind of manual or guide to help me to manage the disorientation and emotional turbulence I was feeling. Something to help me understand what was happening and anticipate what would be coming next. This is part of what motivated me to write this book.

More importantly, I realized in our culture, we are left unaware of a reality which has comforted millions of people grieving the loss of someone they loved . . . the experience of ongoing connection with the one who has departed.

When our society arrives at a place where people finally feel free to share openly their personal experiences of death and what happened after the passing of a loved one, the taboo will be broken. Then, by the time those hearing the stories are dealing with death themselves, they will already be aware of options that will make their way easier, and soften the impact of their loss and grief.

◆   ◆   ◆

If you have been on a similar journey to mine and have lost a loved one, I hope you will see in these pages something that resonates with *your* experience. Something that validates *your* thoughts and feelings. Something that reflects and illuminates the questions, doubts, and insights that *you* may have had at the time.

If, however, you are currently facing the imminent passing of someone you love for the first time, I hope that seeing my journey, and learning from the insights I have gained and share here, will ease your way through the difficult times ahead.

Finally, even if you have not yet been touched by a personal experience of this final transition, you can view this book as an introduction, a kind of preparation, for what you might expect when the inevitable happens and death finds its way into your life, as it most certainly will. It was partly with you in mind that I decided to share my own experience with Shera in some detail in the first chapters.

I invite you to join me on this journey. I hope as happened for me, the changes of "lenses" offered here will make it possible for you to see—in spite of death and grief—the possibility that:

- ◆ Those we have lost do not "die."
- ◆ Our connection with them need not end.
- ◆ Ongoing love and continuing relationship awaits us on the other side of grief.

◆ ◆ ◆

SHERA STREET

DECEMBER 3, 1938—MAY 11, 2020

I HEARD THE WIND...

I heard the wind whispering a secret song
of distant places beyond imagination,
full of Light.
Its hushing voice an irresistible invitation
calling me away
from mind and body,
a siren call drawing me away
from my days and ways,
my thoughts and plans
And I — in spite of myself —
I find I am turning
from my single-minded focus
on staying here
to follow dreams
make plans
and create new projects
... Old stories on repeat in my mind,
defining me,
confining me,
are falling away ....

◆　◆　◆

I will no longer be contained
my curiosity drives me
to find the Source
of this whispering wind.
I feel my Spirit quickening,
The quiet voice of the wind
urges me forward,
farther and farther
faster and faster
Until, at last
at the edge of eternity,
I leap into the void
and fly into forever.

The First Lens — Chaos

Looking through this Lens you will see one of thousands of stories unfolding every day. Stories we generally do not think much about, an inevitable event we seldom plan for. Stories of people coming face to face with a reality everyone in a loving relationship must face at some time: the loss of a person they love.

This first Lens is focussed on one example of such a loss as it unfolds. As common as the story may be in general terms, I invite you to follow me closely as I describe this time. It is my story.

Through this first Lens you meet Shera, my life partner for thirty-four years, and get a sense of our relationship. As I share how we navigated our way through the increasingly serious challenges leading to her passing, I do so, not because they were special or unique, but as a proxy for similar journeys so many people travel, when their health fails over time on the way to death's doorway.

Note for Readers currently experiencing, or who recently have experienced loss: In sharing the intensity of the moments of passing as I experienced them and the days that followed, I am not wishing to distract you from your own experience or dilute it in any way. Rather, I hope my account may offer insights that highlight and validate your own questions and thoughts.

M ost loving relationships grow and expand over time, settling into a form and expression that have a life of their own. In all relationships, at some time, the assumed stability will be challenged and the comfortable sense of permanence that has been taken for granted will come to an end.

This chapter traces an example of this, when a couple at the peak of their lives together and sailing toward an horizon of countless possibilities, first encounter a storm cloud on what seemed to be clear sailing, and then find themselves caught in a succession of storms that eventually sinks their future together entirely.

CHAPTER 1

What Is "Now?"

Crazy times!

Shera, how did we get here? When did it all start?

Who could have known at the beginning where it would lead? So many times you'd be down and then things would start looking better. They'd turn around and you'd be up and running again.

Every time you were hit with a challenge, it was as though you'd say, "Right. So this is what we've got? Now, let's turn it around." And you would! Time and again you'd be up again, living life to the fullest.

"Now" is where you lived. You never seemed to fuss about the past or worry about the future. You just kept focussed on life in the moment and your path of recovery, and the opportunities that each day would bring with every "new now." All the time living life fully. It had always worked—up until now.

What happened this time? We only needed some more time.

Oh Shera, this time, "time" is the one thing we don't have any more.

And this "new now" is for me.

◆　◆　◆

Born a cattle rancher in South Dakota, Shera had lived the life of an artist-adventurer, a healer, and a "mom" to many more than her three sons. She travelled widely and had led tours to Nepal and Bali. For over thirty years, we were the hosts at Serenity by the Sea, a waterfront healing and retreat centre we hand built together, on a small island on Canada's west coast.

NOW KEEPS CHANGING

We had been taking people to Machu Picchu in our twice yearly "Enter the Mystery" tours for eleven years when in 2007, Shera started to encounter health issues.

It started with high blood pressure. As years progressed, and one health challenge followed another, I began to see a pattern. When we got through a challenge, no matter how stable or settled things might then appear to be, they weren't. Many times over months we would think "Okay, now we have resolved the issue," and start to move on, only to find Shera up against some new challenge—a "new now"—and suddenly that would become our new focus.

This ever-evolving ever-changing "now" left us with nothing stable, nothing predictable. We could not say with confidence, "Okay. *Now* that's done. That step is taken. *Now* we can move ahead with that behind us."

As fast as we managed to stabilize an issue in her health, and start to enjoy some months free of concerns, there would be an unexpected event and we would be off on another ride.

It was like crossing water expecting stepping stones, and finding ourselves falling into the river instead.

In retrospect, it is clear that there was never going to be a new "now" that would endure. Perhaps in life there never is. However, as it was unfolding, we didn't recognize that was the case. Even if we had, I doubt things would have changed much.

It was Shera herself who prevented me from internalizing the true seriousness of life-threatening events that came at her over the last eight years. With every crisis and setback her remarkable positivity and resilience would kick in. Over and over, once the situation was handled, Shera would resume her life and we would continue as usual.

Indeed, with her tenacity and positivity, life not only "continued," her passion for life would propel her into another level of expansive activity. From a life-threatening crisis in one moment, to celebrating the joy of living a new adventure in the next: Now we're up, now we're down and now we're up again. There are so many stories! So many "nows."

Let me share an example:

FROM HERO TO HOSPITAL

We lived on Galiano Island, a southern Gulf Island between Vancouver Island and mainland British Columbia. It had only a thousand residents. In September 2011, an extended and exceptionally dry summer had made islanders nervous about possible fires. For several weeks we were regularly cautioning each other to be super vigilant.

After dark one evening, the dreaded call came. Shera and I were told firefighters were battling a fire raging in a waterfront house in our neighbourhood. Firefighters were on the scene. We were told to be aware in case the fire should head our way.

Curious, we hopped into our kayaks and paddled along the shoreline to see for ourselves what was happening. By the time we arrived, the once-magnificent home, atop a seaside cliff was totally engulfed in flames. Other boats were also there. As we watched in horror, it was as though the water itself was aflame with the rippling reflection of the fires above.

I was realizing the hopelessness of the situation, when Shera suddenly shouted, "Look! Over there! The fire is on the hillside!" Unknown to the firefighters above, a brush fire had started at the bottom of the cliff and was starting to burn its way up the forested slope. "We've got to stop it!" This, despite our being in kayaks and having no equipment!

Shera, a woman of action, *always* moved when action was needed. Her urgent words broke the horrified trance the rest of us watching the scene had fallen into and jolted us all into action. Within seconds the boaters had given us empty jerrycans and we were paddling as fast as we could toward the shore.

That is how the two of us ended up, minutes later, sixty feet up the precipitous slope, scrambling across the hillside together, dragging jerrycans now full of water, battling to keep the flames from spreading or reaching into the branches of the trees. Once there, nothing could stop them from raging on into the forest reserve beyond.

As I attacked the higher flames, Shera beat the ground fires down, swinging the jacket she had soaked in seawater—her only "equipment." After an intense forty to forty-five minutes in the smoke and the heat, the flames had been reduced to dying embers on the ground. We had done it! *Now* all was good. We went home pleased and smiling. Shera's heroic action was no surprise to me. In her over seventy years, she always faced challenges full on. I felt flushed and high on our dramatic success.

That high "now" ended a mere three weeks later.

◆　　◆　　◆

"Chidakash, I'm having trouble breathing." Shera woke me in the middle of the night. "I think I have to go to the hospital." I was up like a shot.

Her voice was surprisingly calm, but her words were like an alarm bell. I could never have imagined such words coming from her. I turned immediately to dial 911, glancing at the clock as I did so: 1:10 am.

As I spoke with the dispatcher Shera calmly set about gathering the items from her dresser that she would need for the hospital stay she expected lay ahead. Not wanting to wake me, she had already been up and checking online to understand what was happening to her.

Minutes later we were waiting by the front door for the paramedics to arrive. Although Shera was working hard for her breath, her voice remained calm. It gave a surreal cast to the moment. Given the urgency of the situation and my own elevated state of concern, I was grateful for her quiet manner. I reached to hold her hand.

A small island like Galiano is no place to be caught in a medical emergency. There is no hospital here. After a cursory assessment, the paramedics' first move was to call for a helicopter to airlift Shera to Victoria as fast as possible. Unfortunately, the only one had already been called out to another emergency and was not available.

That is how we ended up sitting in the ambulance at Montague Harbour, a marina further down island, waiting for the arrival of a doctor who had been dispatched in a water ambulance from a location about forty minutes away. I was thankful Shera was holding up. She still seemed remarkably unperturbed by what was clearly a serious and possibly life-threatening issue. The paramedics commented with some relief that my presence seemed to have a stabilizing effect on Shera's life signs. We were still holding hands.

The calm ended however, when the doctor arrived. Evidently wanting to clear the deck for action, he unceremoniously evicted me from the ambulance and turned to examine Shera.

Seconds later, standing at the back of the ambulance, I was suddenly transfixed with horror. Watching through the window, I saw Shera suddenly sit bolt upright, gasping, eyes wide, her arms and hands flailing desperately, grasping at the air in front of her. She looked like she was drowning! She could not breathe! Beside the doctor I could see the oscilloscope on a bench, and was horrified to see the lines tracing the life rhythms of her body bouncing in a crazy scramble across the screen!

The doctor leapt forward to squirt a spray into her mouth. Then he checked the screen. I was in a panic. Only six feet—and a lifetime—away from where Shera was struggling in such distress. I was locked outside, my heart wrenching. I felt utterly helpless.

"Dear God! Shera, this is not the way this is supposed to be! Anytime I have thought of the time death would come to us, I had resolved to be beside you—holding your hand. Not like this!"

Again, the doctor leapt forward with the spray. Shera looked even more desperate! Again and again the doctor sprayed, throwing caution to the wind; each time checking the erratic lines bouncing across the screen for some sign of improvement. Spray, and then spray again! Clearly, he had no other option.

Then, as suddenly as it had begun, the crisis was over. Shera caught a breath, then took another and another. Her flailing hands dropped to her lap and she settled back onto the gurney. As her face calmed, the lines on the screen settled back into to a normal array of pulsing rhythms.

EMERGENCY, NO EMERGENCY.

The boat continued to a marina at Swartz Bay, where Shera's gurney was wheeled up the dock to a waiting ambulance. Surprisingly, throughout the whole process and in the ambulance ride to the hospital, Shera was quite normal and upbeat. She made no reference to her experience.

In the emergency room, doctors immediately set to work assessing her condition. She had suffered a catastrophic heart failure. Her heart was able to pump only a fraction of the blood it was supposed to move. She had felt a shortness of breath because the oxygen she needed was not being delivered to her cells. After several hours of tests and rest, the doctors were confident her condition had stabilized. They decided she would stay the night in the hospital as a precaution. They'd check on her status in the morning.

The next morning, unsure what I would find, I arrived early, anxious to know how Shera had spent the night. I entered her room and discovered her sitting up in the bed, looking radiant, the light above her causing her hair to glow like a halo. As I entered, Shera looked up, her eyes sparkling, and smiled brightly. Always the artist, she was happily occupied drawing away in her ever-present little sketchbook. There was not a hint of the extraordinary events of the previous twenty-four hours. Surreal. Wonderful!

When she had been cleared to leave and had gotten dressed, I sent her down to the parking lot with a young friend to wait for me while I finished up with the doctors. Minutes later, when I got to the parking lot to join them, I found Shera standing at the back of the truck, on one leg, arms intertwined in front of her face, demonstrating the eagle pose to our young friend in an impromptu yoga class! Having just left the doctors, it's hard to describe the effect this image had on my mind. It's as though all we had just gone through hadn't happened. By appearances, the "now" I thought I was dealing with had changed from near-death to totally normal. I had to laugh. And to think she had been fighting a forest fire three weeks earlier!

Shera saw me approaching and smiled, "This is a chance to stop at Salt Spring on the way home to see how things are going with my studio." We had bought a property on Salt Spring, a neighbouring island, and Shera had immediately started the building even before we had sold Serenity by the Sea. She wanted to be able to hit the ground running, whenever we finally moved there.

Never one to let an opportunity go to waste, Shera was not going to miss this chance to check on progress.

She said not a word about her experience. "Now" was all there was.

PLANNING THE FUTURE NOW

A couple of hours and a ferry ride later, I'm in our parking lot on Salt Spring, watching Shera conferring with her builder and the plumber. She is standing in the middle of the construction site, surrounded by rebar and the formwork being readied for pouring the foundation. As I observe them, I am distracted by someone who has arrived unnoticed and is walking up to me. It is Ben, a friend, and I am a little puzzled to notice a look of concern on his face.

"Chidakash, I'm so sorry," he says earnestly. Then, taking my outstretched hand in his, "I just heard about Shera." His back is turned to the work site.

In the middle of his commiseration about what I must be going through, Shera steps up beside us. She has left her conference and made her way across the formwork to ask me a question. Briefly greeting Ben, she turns to ask me the question. Then, armed with my answer, she turned to rejoin the others.

When I looked back again to Ben, I see his eyes are locked on Shera, now picking her way over the obstacle course of rebar on her way back to the middle of the worksite where the two men are waiting for her. Ben looks like he's in a trance. His mouth has dropped open.

"Um . . . Ben, what's happening?" I ask.

As he turns his face toward me to reply, his voice has a strange quality, as though he speaking to himself, reciting an automatic message in his head.

"Two years ago, the doctors told me I had a serious congenital heart defect and that I could die at any time." He had used to be an active outdoorsman.

"And so, you haven't done anything for two years since then?"

He raised his eyes to meet mine, paused, and nodded his head.

❖ And then I understood: this man in his mid-thirties had suspended his life for two years in fear that each day may be his last. He is trying to make sense of a finding seventy-two-year-old woman who has just barely survived catastrophic heart failure a day and a half ago, standing in the middle of a building site, working on her future studio gallery, a dream project only she can see. Not just planning her future, she is actively building it. *Now.*

Shera hadn't missed a beat.

EVER A TRAVELLER

There's more. For eighteen years, Shera and I had led tours together to Machu Picchu in the high mountains of Peru one or two times a year. At the time of this crisis, we were within weeks of setting out on our fall tour. We had to address the implications of this new "now" we were in.

Despite appearances, and Shera's remarkable resilience and positivity, we both knew the congestive heart failure was real. Shera's heart was only functioning at twenty-five to thirty percent of normal and had a troubling irregularity of rhythm. Any exertion requiring more oxygen could precipitate another crisis. Certainly, flying or travelling to higher altitudes where the air is rarified was out of the question.

At any age, let alone the age of seventy-two, we knew heart failure meant that she would not be joining me on the tour in the high mountains this time. I was very concerned and didn't want to leave Shera at home alone so soon after her emergency. However, she was adamant that we not cancel the tour, and with her urging I went on to Peru for the first time without her, leaving her behind on Galiano Island.

Five days later, I arrived in Peru, in Cusco, with my group. As soon as I'd settled them into our hotel, I headed down to the computers in the foyer to check for messages online, hoping to find word from

Galiano. I was pleased to see an email from Shera, and immediately opened it, keen to see how—*she was in Hawaii!?* My goodness! I certainly wasn't expecting that! Apparently, she had gotten bored at home and had decided to visit her son Spar on Maui.

Then I opened the photos she had attached to the email. I could hardly believe my eyes! Even knowing Shera is a champion of the unexpected, this was beyond outrageous. Among photos with the family, several showed her walking on a slackline strung above a sparkling blue swimming pool—*naked*!

That's how it was with Shera. It was yet another "now." I had left her at home knowing she was barred from travelling in the high altitudes of Peru, never suspecting she would simply re-set her travel options to sea level destinations, in the process ignoring the risk of the air travel itself.

Upon reflection, I imagine that in spite of her cavalier demeanour, following the run to the hospital, Shera fully understood the implications of the crisis she had just survived. I realized the priority for her was to see her son and his family again. Ironically, although she totally understood she couldn't go trekking at high altitude in the mountains, she had not registered that air travel was also a risk for someone with her diagnosis. Shera always moved on impulse. Thankfully there was no problem.

With her eyes on the future she intended to live, Shera was planning to indulge her primary passions of painting and gardening—and loving her family. This was something that held true through every challenge. After this and every subsequent crisis, Shera managed to create a highlight in her life.

Within a year, her large studio gallery was built and stocked with enough frames and canvasses for an army, and in the next year she had doubled the size of an already sizeable vegetable garden.

◆　　◆　　◆

NOW

For the following seven or eight years the shadow of the unthinkable had become part of our lives, popping in and out every year or two. Over that time there had been many crises that took us to the emergency room. Occasional runs to the hospital had effectively become a part of our lifestyle. We drove ourselves there and were transported there by ambulance, water ambulance, and even helicopter. The issues had always been resolved or put on hold. Even though the physical issues we were coping with seemed to keep compounding, it would have felt like a betrayal if I were to believe *this* time would be any different.

I believe Shera felt the same way. We never talked about death as such. Our unspoken agreement was to focus always on recovery, and Shera never missed an opportunity to move to the positive.

A perfect example of this was in 2015 on Christmas Eve. I had surprised Shera with a special treat: tickets to see the Nutcracker Suite performed by the Bolshoi Ballet. She was delighted! It had always been one of her favourites. The performance was to be broadcast live on a Saturday evening from Moscow, which meant on Salt Spring Island we would be viewing it on Saturday morning. To be there in the morning we had to catch the Friday afternoon ferry from Galiano and stay overnight. We went to bed that night with great anticipation.

We had barely gone to sleep when Shera woke again. She was having great difficulty breathing. Fortunately, Salt Spring is a much larger island *with* a hospital. As an added blessing, given the urgency, it was only a mile away. We had no need to lose precious moments waiting for an ambulance, and I was able to drive her to the hospital myself. We arrived with Shera in severe distress. Thankfully, once an oxygen mask had been put on her face the crisis quickly passed. I believe her angels were working overtime. If we had *not* happened to be on Salt Spring, I believe the story would have ended there.

The next morning, having slept well and feeling better, Shera wanted to go to the ballet—of course! She immediately started floating the idea with the doctors that she be granted a pass to leave the hospital for two hours. The doctor was surprised by the request of course, but after a moment or two he was open to the idea. If something should happen with Shera, the theatre was only a two-to-three-minute drive away. He agreed. Another small triumph.

Afterward, back in the hospital, flushed with having enjoyed the show, we learned the doctors had decided Shera needed a level of care she could only receive from the larger Royal Jubilee Hospital in Victoria. That is how on Christmas Eve, she found herself once again cross-strapped onto a gurney, being airlifted in a helicopter to a hospital in Victoria.

Totally at ease in spite of the situation, Shera gazed down at the brightly lit night streets far below us. She delighted herself and the nurse accompanying us, with a sudden thought, "Look! We are riding in Santa's sleigh!" We all laughed. As always, Shera was taking it in her stride, now at the ballet, and now in a medical evacuation helicopter.

In the Victoria hospital it was determined that she needed a pacemaker. However, the time to clear paperwork to import the required device from Germany meant she would spend the next two months in hospital, wired to a heart monitor. Shera calmly settled in, content to spend her days perched on her hospital bed, a pen or brushes in hand, focussed on her artwork in front of her. Another "now."

Over the following days and weeks, Shera turned her room into an art gallery. Remarkably, with her angels obviously still at work, she had been given a private room and I was able to stay with her. For two months she painted and drew. We received friends, and enjoyed the music of some of them who were musicians and had brought their instruments. We even had a surprise birthday party for a friend!

At one point with three friends in the room, one of them picked up his guitar and started singing and playing. The other two got up to dance. Unable to contain herself, Shera, who has always been an irrepressible dancer, set her artwork aside and hopped out of bed to join in. Less than a half a minute later, the door of the room burst open! Three nurses exploded into the room, faces forward, eyes open wide. We had forgotten that the electrodes and wires linking Shera's chest to the heart monitor were also linked to a display at the nursing station outside. When the lines suddenly started leaping across their screen, the nurses came running, thinking that Shera was having a siezure! We all laughed. Shera was undaunted.

"CONFOUNDING PROGNOSIS"

There were several occasions when it was clear that doctors had already written her off. First it was the heart failure, and that had been followed two years later with a diagnosis of cancer. Yet despite the odds, she would tap into some fount of resilience and rebound, and we would resume our lives.

Indeed. Her heart had recovered its function beyond all expectations and was on the lower threshold of the normal range, and the cancer was in remission. Upon hearing the news from the doctor about her heart's recovery, I can remember her dancing a brief jig in the examin-ation room. Then, eyes sparkling, she took the hand of the bewildered doctor in hers, set her foot beside his and challenged him to an Indian wrestle, where each person tries to pull the other off balance. She was irrepressible. It seemed now things were stabilizing at last. Her family doctor told her once with huge admiration, "Shera, you have a way of confounding prognosis."

Then, two years later, at the age of seventy-eight, another catastro-phe struck when Shera was in hospital again for an operation to reset a broken ankle. The operation was rescheduled day by day until the third day. During this time, Shera was taken off the blood thinners which had been preventing blood clots and associated risks since her heart failure. The successive delays proved to be a tragic mismanagement by the hospital. The operation was finally performed on the third day, However, without the blood thinners to protect her, Shera fell victim to a massive stroke.

In the hallway of the hospital after another surgery which had failed to remove the clot in her brain, I was told by the surgeon Shera would lose all capacity to speak. Nothing spoken or written or signed would be understood by her. Devastating news.

Yet it was only moments before Shera proved his prognosis wrong.

As we were speaking, a gurney carrying Shera emerged from the operating room beside us. I turned immediately and went to stand beside her. She was lying on her back, eyes wide open, goggle-eyed, evidently not seeing anything in particular. I leaned forward and looked down into her face. I said to her softly, "Shera, have I told you lately that I love you?" Her eyes gathered themselves enough to turn to mine. Her mouth opened, her lips rounding to form a silent word, "No."

This question had always been a special game between us. "Lately" was never late enough, so for us the correct answer was always, "No." Shera had understood my question and had communicated the correct response.

Yet the doctor failed to take note—I was to be told two more times that there was no possibility of Shera receiving or giving any communication at all.

The head of the neurology department was so confident of this distressing prognosis, that he delivered it to me across the hospital bed on which Shera was lying. Her head, eyes closed, was resting on the pillow *between us*, inches away from him! She could hear everything he said. I was shocked. However, Shera's expression never changed.

Having made his pronouncement, the doctor then turned to leave. When the door closed behind him, I turned back to Shera. Now her bright eyes were looking directly into mine, with the light of an ironic smile in them. She then scrunched her face up, mouth twisted, to deliver an unmistakable, ironic message: "Who the hell was *that?*" Shera's son Jib, who had witnessed the whole thing from the foot of the bed, joined me in a burst of laughter. Shera was having none of it!

❖ Shera did not listen to limiting thoughts from doctors. Her determination and her recovery were both inspiring and exciting. Her movement, coordination, ability to speak, spell, read and even type, all progressed far beyond anything we were told by the doctors to hope for. Yet five months later she was talking, painting again, and working in her garden. It was impossible. It was inspiring. A new now.

Then fate turned again. A misdiagnosis failed to recognize the beginning of the cancer's return, and by the time it was properly identified, it had another ten months to progress.

We embarked on an exhaustive search for therapies.

◆　◆　◆

We continued as always, neither of us willing to concede that any given challenge could indeed be her last in this life. We had an unspoken bond built on the unshakeable belief in her ultimate recovery, and the resilience that had brought her back from so many challenges in the past.

This was in evidence in one visit with her family doctor. Shera was sitting directly in front of him. Believing that this time Shera was on a one-way street so to speak, the doctor asked if she would be okay with him sharing a process he had learned at a recent conference, which would help patients prepare for imminent end of life. He was intending to offer it as support.

I was sitting to the side as he introduced the topic, and I was a bit taken aback when he described what he had in mind. This topic had never been part of any of our consultations before.

I had long established my role as Shera's advocate, and after her stroke impacted her ability to find the words she wanted to say, I would answer, on her behalf, most of the questions she was asked. She would let me know if I was off the mark. This time, however, I remember distinctly choosing to keep my mouth shut. I continued to sit quietly. This was her question to answer, and I wanted to hear what she would say.

To my surprise she agreed immediately. Moreover, she did so with her characteristic enthusiasm, leaning forward in her chair, curious, a smile on her face, as always open to receiving something new.

The doctor showed some relief and began to speak. However, he had gotten no further than a couple of sentences when Shera, interrupted him to say that this was not what she wanted to hear. Simply, showing no distress, and as a matter of fact, she let him know that she had misunderstood what he was offering. Clearly, she had not yet changed her intention to recover. What the doctor saw as her imminent death was not where she was going to put her attention or her energy.

SEARCHING, SEARCHING

It was so hard to hold this current unfolding reality of health challenges alongside all the adventures we had shared, especially when the challenges had always seemed to resolve and release us to new adventures. I doubted I would ever get a coherent picture of it all in my head.

With this new challenge of the return of her cancer, I embarked on a search for healing options. I quickly discovered an endless variety of possible healing agents and treatments. They had come to my attention in many ways: through the internet, social media, and by word of mouth from friends. Holistic, energetic, naturopathic, homeotherapeutic, supplements, and diet. I was open to everything.

❖ And they came together with an ongoing rat's nest of issues to sort out. Anything not certified by Western and pharmaceutical medicine was inevitably questioned or discredited outright on their websites and organizational platforms. It seemed as soon as I found something relevant and promising, I would immediately discover with further checking, some medical "authority" warning of hoaxes or contraindications: "Do not use with high blood pressure," or, "Do not use if taking blood thinners." It was an ongoing frustration to believe that, just out of reach, was something that could resolve all the problems, and Shera would recover.

I gained a real appreciation for the dilemma facing doctors. No one, especially practicing doctors, can stay on top of all the new options and chemical cocktails that are the lifeblood of Western medicine, let alone track the relative value and interventions possible through alternative medicine.

I was mining cancertutor.org daily for information. We had embarked on different protocols with funny names: Budwig, Celect. I was always open to learning more about anything from physical and holistic, to energetic and spiritual. We were both enthralled to hear Joe Dispenza describing accounts of people who had miraculous healing by working in the pure energy of the Quantum Field.

Miracles were tantalizingly close. At one point, in December 2019, Shera had been dealing with a high level of pain for much of an evening. Shera's son, Spar, who had flown in from Hawaii to spend Christmas with us, suggested we call his friend Bob, a psychic healer on the East Coast.

Bob listened as I briefly explained what was happening. Then he said, "I'm on it" and hung up.

We sat anxiously with Shera, and miraculously, within four or five minutes, her pain suddenly lessened and then went away completely. She was okay again! We were blown away and immediately the flames of hope grew brighter in us. Although occasionally in the following months pain would reappear, it was not often, and it was never that bad again.

We continued in this mode for five months, hoping against hope, in spite of Shera's obvious decline, which continued to intensify. In her final weeks, I was told by another psychic healer that Shera's physical, mental, and emotional bodies were seriously degraded to the point of collapse. Her spiritual body, however, was shining. I was not surprised.

I believe all these modalities of healing are valid and can be effective. That they ultimately did not work in our case could have been because we started too late, or I did not understand or properly apply the remedies I found.

A BIGGER PLAN

❖ In a way we were covering all our options. Over Shera's final weeks, even as we continued the search for a way to turn this situation around, we were also continuing to imagine our future, *and* I was finding ways to revisit her past. On the one hand, I would create meditations and play video documentaries about elephants and nature and things she loved, and the safaris we planned to take in Africa.

❖ On the other hand, I celebrated her past and her accomplishments. In meditations and prayers, I gave thanks for all she had faced and overcome. I acknowledged her body for all it had given her and the many places it had taken her. I played videos taking her back to her beginnings on a sprawling cattle ranch in South Dakota; videos of rodeos, cattle drives, wild horses, and horsemanship.

In retrospect, this work I was doing with Shera added a profound dimension to these weeks. I came to feel the fullness of our life and dreams—what we had shared and what we planned for—in a way that was almost tangible. Despite the daily evidence of Shera's increasing decline, during our sessions, I often found myself in a place of profound gratitude that I had never known before.

In our meditations, even as I called on angels for healing, I would voice three assertions:

- ◆ We willingly accept whatever the future will bring us because
- ◆ We believe there are no mistakes in the universe, and
- ◆ We know that there is always a "Bigger Plan"

DO NOT RESUSCITATE

Subsequently, the approach of Shera's doctor shifted. At one point I was given a "Do Not Resuscitate" form that was delivered by a home care nurse. I was supposed to fill it out and have it on hand. I remember holding it in my hands and looking at it, resisting the implications.

As an idea, as something to be done, it was hardly unexpected or hard to imagine. Yet after so many years and so many crises and so many miraculous recoveries, how could I now be contemplating such a thing? While my hands started to fill out the form, I could feel my resentment building. How could I suspend my belief in what I felt was still possible. And I felt something else . . . in filling in Shera's name it felt as if I was engaging in an act of betrayal. We had spent years, and all of our treatment hours for months, focussing on recovery. Why couldn't we create yet another turnaround? Yes, it was a long shot, but why couldn't Shera bounce back as she always had?

I put the form aside. Not now.

DEATH CERTIFICATE

Then, as we continued, I was told that Shera would no longer be given blood transfusions; news I found profoundly disturbing. Clearly now others were making decisions which assumed Shera was not going to be able to continue. She would no longer be offered the help that had been instantly available whenever she needed it . . . up to now.

That was hard to take. There had been such solid support for so long, it felt strange to find it being withdrawn, piece by piece. Yet another "new now." This one had dark and unsettling implications. In spite of all we tried, a day came when the home care nurse gave me an envelope. It was from the hospice support team. I opened it to find it contained a blank death certificate. A *death* certificate!? For someone who had been so alive?

That's the way it was. There is a kind of momentum; an assumption of continuity—that what has been will continue to be—that we can continue to rinse and repeat. That our ability to create new "nows" could continue endlessly . . .

Each time I looked, something else would have changed: I'd find another link to check out, an issue that required attention, another cure, a new expectation, a habit that had to change, an appointment to make. What I was dealing with in any given moment was changing so fast, I was having trouble keeping track. It is hard to find a path across a fast-flowing river.

Now, suddenly, I had to put this current dreadful reality alongside all the adventures we had shared. It would be a long while, if ever, before I would get this all sorted in my head. I needed some answers to the questions that were surfacing in my mind. What was happening?

A WOMAN'S PREROGATIVE

The end of April 2020, I asked Shera, "We're still on the path to recovery, right?" Her response was an immediate nod, "Yes!"

However, five days later, she was unable to take her pills, or even swallow water. After our last attempt, I left her to rest for a while. When I returned to check on her, her face was turned to the wall. I went around the bed to stand in front of her. For the first time ever, Shera did not register my presence. Her eyes did not rise to meet mine. Expressionless, they remained fixed on the blank wall before her.

She had changed her mind. She was ready to move on.

I understood immediately. In that instant, *everything* changed. From that moment I was no longer in the mode that I had been in for almost two years, focussed solely on how to integrate her meds, supplements, treatments, rehab and exercise, meals, and body care, and program them all into the day.

I realized all of my efforts had failed to put her on a path to recovery. I had no choice but to accept that. I had been moving from day to day for so long, I was on automatic. Each day simply doing what was necessary, now this, now that, mostly a repetition of tasks. Giving treatments, administering medications, bathing, preparing food. It was a routine that had continued for over a year, gradually intensifying month by month. It had encouraged a mesmerizing disconnect at some level from the understanding of what was actually happening in front of me: namely that Shera was on an overarching trajectory toward an inevitable outcome.

As I write this, I am amazed at how readily I had accepted her decision. It was clear to me she had accepted she was beyond miracles to save. All the reference points and the patterns that had given shape to our days together had disappeared. She was willing to surrender to a "Bigger Plan."

In that moment there was no way I could have looked around and found my bearings. Nothing was stable. "Now" had lost its meaning. It felt like I had been thrown into a whirlpool.

THE END OF NOWS

We had finally entered a zone of transition. A strange time that has no game plan. A time which follows no rules. A moment I had known may come. I had no idea of when or how it would arrive or what it would look like. It had always been in the future, and now I was in the middle of it, a strange, almost tangible, indefinable moment that had a momentum of its own. Somehow, I had to find a way of moving with it.

I wonder what it was like for Shera. That moment of decision. She, too, would be aware of her choice. That she had changed her mind. That she had released her indefatigable determination to continue on. In spite of the magnitude of the decision, I expect when it was before her at last, she came to it easily and without regret. She always had faced whatever challenges life had thrown her way, accepting what was truly beyond her control, and continuing on. This time, "continuing on" took on a completely new meaning.

So, when this moment came, I realized that my role as caretaker healer had changed in an instant. All the energy and activities that had dominated our days for months was released. Now my role was to stay by her, reassuring her that she was not alone, and seeing her safely on her way. I saw myself as a protector and resolved to guide her safely to her next step.

❖ I dedicated my energy and my actions to loving her, letting her know she was loved, and clearing the way for her departure. Now, the only service that I could offer Shera was to ease her passing. For me, that meant helping to alleviate any fear or apprehension she might have, and encouraging her to embrace this next step. A step that would free her from a body no longer able to sustain her spirit in this world so, figuratively speaking, she could spread her wings and fly off into a bigger Reality.

ZOOM

Shera had three sons she loved deeply. Spar in Hawaii, Jib in North Carolina and Robert in California. She was godmother to a girl and a boy (now adults) in Peru, whom she cherished, and as such had become a beloved part of their families. I called them all to let them know that Shera was about to leave us. I was concerned Shera would not be able to have her families with her in these, her final days, to say goodbye, because of both the considerable distances involved, and the restrictions governments were imposing all travel during the pandemic. Then I thought of Zoom, the online meeting space.

❖ Why could it not be used to create a family vigil with an ongoing Zoom meeting by Shera's bedside? Within a couple of hours, Shera's entire family was with her . . . virtually . . . within a couple of feet of her pillow. From Hawaii, California, North Carolina, and Peru. Shera had the loves of her life in front of her.

She could hear their quiet words of comfort reassuring her.

It was remarkable. For seven days, as she rested and drifted, Shera had only to lift her eyes to know all the sweet souls whom she loved so much were with her, and see their earnest faces, love beaming from their eyes.

This continued with the Zoom call being closed for only a few hours, from late at night to the early morning so we could all get some sleep.

With no idea how long this vigil would continue, I had been pleased to discover during this time, we had spent Mother's Day with Shera surrounded virtually by her entire family, loving and honouring her. Perhaps that's why she had stayed with us so many days.

Then I began to wonder if there was some other reason. I remembered the psychic healer that had worked on Shera a couple of days before her decision to leave. She had said Shera was challenged in her mental, emotional, and physical bodies. Only her spiritual body was shining brightly. She reported that Shera's "higher self" was embracing her leaving. She had also added another message, "Shera is staying for two reasons: she feels the shame of dying, and she feels the need to give a message to one of her sons."

❖ With that in mind, I suggested that each of us speak with her privately to clear away any unfinished business that may have been holding her here for all these days, and release her to fly on. We followed the process of Ho'oponopono, a teaching that originates in Hawaii. It holds that healing and release occurs between people if we can share these four sentiments:

Please forgive me for any injury or distress that I have caused you.
I forgive you for any injury or distress that you have caused me.
Thank you for who you are and all you have given me.
I love you.

To these I added two additional statements:

Don't worry. I am able to look after myself and I'll be okay if you choose to leave.
I release you.

Clearly, we succeeded in giving Shera what she needed to go. The next day was the seventh day of the vigil, and it became Shera's final day. It continued much as the others, with gentle music, and Shera drifting in and out of semi-consciousness, her eyes parting slightly at times to register that her family was with her.

Until the late afternoon. The final step only lasted half an hour. Her breathing quickened and her diaphragm worked harder. And then it stopped. At the time she died, when it was clear that her breathing was done, her eyes looked up to mine. She wanted to hear the mantra again that I'd repeated over and over again through those days: "You are okay, I am with you, I will stay by your side. Don't be afraid. You are not alone. Your family is with you." This one last time I said, "You're at the Door. You have done so well."

As Shera took her leave, I felt only gratitude that she had been granted the grace of such a quiet and gentle passing. An artist, healer, and traveler, she had spent her life living so many adventures. She considered the eagle to be her power animal and herself as an eagle woman. I could almost see her spreading her wings as she moved through the Door. "Now," after years in a body less and less able, Shera's Spirit was free at last, and flying into a new adventure beyond anything she could imagine or hope for.

Death may be anticipated for days, weeks or even longer, with focus and emotions intensifying the whole time, creating a bubble that envelops all concerned. Yet the moment it arrives is the instant it is over.

The bubble bursts. It is as though a huge in-breath has suddenly been released. The surreality of it all can be a gift and has the power to suspend thought and set pain and grief aside for the time being.

The time of someone's passing is a time when, numbed to all but the moment, subtle imperatives take us through the first steps that need to be taken.

CHAPTER 2

What Just Happened!?

NOTICE OF DEPARTURE

Shera left us in the evening (May 11th), sweetly, and with magnificent grace, to shine her Light in a new place.

It was beautiful, and comforting beyond measure to have had the whole family together at my side—virtually, via Zoom—from Hawaii, California, North Carolina and Peru, loving her and releasing her to her next adventure. For six days she had been without food or water, continuing on, her eyes closed or almost closed, opening only intermittently; conscious and resting, preparing herself to go. On the seventh and final day, her eyes were open the entire day. They seemed to be soaking in the love beaming from the faces on the screen before her, all those special souls that she loves so much. I think she wanted to take that image away with her—being bathed in their love. Shera showed no fear. No distress. Conscious to the end. Such a noble and gentle way to take her leave. Such grace.

I am so very grateful for the days and days we were all gifted to be with her as she made her way all the way to the final Door, right up where she opened it, gently spread her wings and flew on.

I am so very proud of her.

I feel fulfilled and grateful. I have been profoundly blessed.

◆   ◆   ◆

Shera, I wish you a bon voyage. You've probably arrived already where you are going, and I hope you've had a chance to catch your breath. Whenever you happen to look back here, I hope you are enjoying all the creativity that is taking place in your name.

I want you to know that if and when the storm clouds of difficult times come my way, when I look at the sky, you will be the silver lining I am looking for.

◆   ◆   ◆

After Shera passed, I sat quietly by her bedside, with the members of her far-flung family still present on the screen beside me. We sat together in silence. Nothing was said for quite a while, each caught in our own thoughts at what had just happened. Without it being spoken, I felt all of us were touched the sacredness of the moment, the gift of what we had experienced. Then we began sharing some of our thoughts. It was comforting to feel connection with each other, in spite of the thousands of miles that separated us from each other.

AFTERMATH

Over the next three hours, our families bonded with each other through our love of Shera. Shera's sons and their families in Hawaii, California, and North Carolina expressed their love and appreciation to her "heart" families, her godchildren in Peru, for being an important part of Shera's life. All of us felt linked through the sharing of our lives and love with the woman who had just left us.

Each of us spoke in turn of the experience we had just shared, Shera's presence was in everything we did and said. In these first hours after her passing, during the precious time the family spent sharing our thoughts and our love, I could sense that Shera was somewhere not too far away.

Then we bade each other good night. In Hawaii Spar ended the Zoom call, and I shut down my computer.

❖ The evening reminded me of something I realized during the deaths of my parents. The final gift a departing loved one can give those they are leaving is one of life's rare opportunities to bear witness when they leave. They can experience and be touched by a Mystery that has captivated the imagination and wonder since the beginning of humankind. A chance to glimpse the Essence of who we really are as living Souls.

At such a transition, time and the world drops away. Differences and contentions that may divide us can lose their power. We are given an opportunity to rediscover what is important in life, and connect authentically, heart to heart. Reconnection is possible.

After I shut down the computer, silence settled into the room around me. Alone, I continued sitting beside the bed where Shera's body lay, experiencing the solitude. I was trying to fathom what had happened. As much as I had thought I knew what was coming, what to expect, I found myself instead in the presence of a profound Mystery. I was filled with questions I could not put into words. Although I didn't know it in these terms at the time, the seeds were planted in me that were to grow into a quest to understand what I had just experienced in Shera's passing.

When I turned once again to her body, this dear manifestation that had always *been* Shera for all the years we were together, I could not see Shera there. It still amazes me that as I sat alone, in the silent room in this moment, with the irrevocable loss of the woman I loved undeniably proven by her body lying on the bed before me, it was no longer *Shera*.

❖ It was her *body*. Something intangible had changed. That was when I realized I was seeing the difference when Spirit leaves the body. Once her essence, her life force, was no longer present in her body, *enlivening* it, I could see in some clear and literal sense, the body was no longer *her* and no longer looked like her.

I believe over the previous seven days, I really did internalize that Shera's spirit was leaving its physical temple and had flown on; that her body was simply that: a gift on loan from the Earth, which was about to be returned. Perhaps I had just mesmerized myself into the belief that she had indeed passed through some "Door".

I was struck with a profound wonder that this now so obviously empty shell had been the vehicle that had carried her through all the days and years, adventures and experiences of her eighty-one years here. I felt the desire to honour this "vessel," now empty, for all it had been when filled with the life essence and vitality of my sweetheart.

In that moment I imagined how, in earlier times and other places, families of loved ones who gathered to be with someone at the time of their passing might have bathed the body together.

I put on some music that we both loved and then ran warm water into a shallow basin. While the music played, I bathed her body, my hand guiding the cloth over first one and then another of the hands, arms, and feet that would no longer be in my life.

❖ I felt no resistance inside. No sadness. No remorse . . . I felt *gratitude*.

There was a special gift for me in moving my hands one last time over the body I had loved for so many years. A sense of completion. Washing, and then towelling the body dry. I realized in some spontaneous alchemy, this act of bathing became a sacred ceremony through which I could fully internalize—and accept—that this body that Shera and I had both tried so hard to save was now inert. Beyond saving. Shera had left.

❖   ❖   ❖

After completing the bathing, I felt the desire to dress Shera's body. I had barely begun when Bob and Marianne, a husband and wife team from the funeral home arrived at the door.

During the past week I had alerted the funeral home to the situation, and before I had started to bathe Shera's body, I had phoned to let them know she had passed.

It was now very late in the evening. Although technically they were dispatched to collect a body and deliver it to the morgue, thankfully, they were in no rush. Sensitive and supportive, they were an exceptional team. They clearly understood the importance of what I was doing and offered to assist me.

❖ As I dressed her, I was focussed on acknowledging and serving this body one final time, and I experienced this exercise as a gift. I felt a surprising peacefulness as I worked. It was such a gentle way to internalize that Shera had indeed "left", a sense reinforced, paradoxically, by the feeling I had of Shera's presence with me in the room.

With the task done, and Shera's body properly honoured, I had the impulse to record the image with a photograph. I had no clear reason for this at the time. Perhaps I felt the moment was too important to risk forgetting the details. Perhaps the drab hospital garb had been too much of an insult to the creative flare Shera put into how she dressed: in her choice of fabric, colour, and design, and needed to be gone. More likely I understood at some level it might serve anyone in Shera's families unable to get the closure they needed, without viewing the body in person, as could have happened if they had been able to travel. The photograph would be a kind of substitute. Now they would see 'Shera' in her favourite garments, which they would have seen her wearing many times.

Afterward, in looking at the pictures, I was struck again at how dramatically evident it was that the body was not Shera. Her clothes had always been a playful expression of her vibrancy and creativity. Yet even with these special garments once again adorning Shera's body, they failed completely to create an illusion of its *being* her. I could understand the challenge for undertakers to attempt the task of making a dead body appear to be alive and sleeping.

Afterward, we placed Shera's body on the gurney that had been rolled into the room. I felt my heart catch momentarily as I watched the black shroud—*why black Shera? You always insisted on colour!*—was drawn over the body, and a flap pulled up to cover the face I loved so much. It was so strange to see her face being covered! Such a simple thing that would never be done while she was alive.

I followed as Bob guided the gurney out of the house and wheeled it over to the sleek black van in the parking lot. Then he opened the hatchback. I felt an odd twist inside as I watched them put the gurney, with its precious cargo inside the vehicle—*a hearse*. It was the last time that dear body which had been Shera's, would leave the home we had shared, its destination: the morgue—*my god! It's going to the morgue!*

ALONE

After watching the black vehicle make its way up the driveway, merging with the black of the night in pursuit of the light cast by its headlights, I turned back into the house. It was now one o'clock in the morning.

When I got to the bedroom, I stepped through the doorway and halted. I had been stopped by the scene before me. The bright ceiling lights highlighted the garish disorder that was now *my* bedroom. In the centre of the room stood the hospital bed that had been occupied by Shera, empty. Beside it was the single bed I had used so I could sleep by her side. Both were in disarray. Scattered around them were all the bits and pieces—basins clothes, towels, monitors—that had been so important in the hours and days just passed. Now they meant nothing at all.

I stood there in shock at the sight of a room in which I had been immersed for days. For weeks it had been like a cauldron filled with surging energy and emotions; it had contained the focussed intensity of non-stop presence and love of Shera's families; and it had held Shera herself, the catalyst at centre of it all, quietly preparing for her departure. All of it was now gone. I could feel their absence still echoing in the glaring emptiness and total silence of the room.

Despite the late hour, I set about changing the energy, and started with the considerable task of disassembling the hospital bed. It had been such a welcome aid and exactly the support Shera and I needed when it arrived. Yet now, standing in the middle of the chaos, it seemed to mock the situation. From the beginning it had implied the outcome I had just experienced, not the recovery we had hoped for. It had to go.

An hour later, the bed had been completely taken apart and moved to the front hallway. Then I turned to the clutter that had gathered in the corners of the room and put it put it all out of sight. Finally, I swept and mopped the floor. Then I changed the sheets and made my bed.

As I worked, at times I felt a vague discomfort. It seemed too soon for me to be doing this—was I trying to clean *Shera* out of the room? Was it really so simple? "Here one moment, gone the next." "Time to move on?"

It seemed so cold and unloving.

Although the thought pushed at me, trying to draw me in, I let it go. The greater insult would have been to leave the room as it was: a temporary shrine to her departure. No. She was gone. I gained no comfort in prolonging that experience, continuing to endure her passing. I was simply taking the next step that had to be taken.

When I was done, I turned out the light and climbed into bed.

I was alone.

I did not really understand what had happened, and I had no idea what lay ahead.

◆　◆　◆

This chapter introduces the three phases of loss. It shows how, in spite of the fear we may have of death, death itself is not the biggest challenge a survivor deals with. When death is expected but it's not known when, the waiting can be so emotionally distressing that when it comes, death may be experienced as a release on both sides.

When death is expected, often the major challenges come in the days, weeks, and even months *after* a death, when the survivor is navigating the emotional confusion and disorientation of their new reality and managing the practical demands that are part of it.

CHAPTER 3

Impossibly Real—My Quest Begins

THE LOSS OF YOU

I feel the loss of you
    in the hole punched through our dreams
        in the rent torn across the fabric
            of our life together

I feel my heart break
    to see your gallery without you
        your garden waiting in vain
            the greenhouse empty
I ache at your absence now
    from the spaces we have shared
        in our home
            in our lives
Over these past few challenging years
    you had become more and even more
        the centre of my life's focus
            the heart of my heart

my pivot point

   the lynch pin of my life

I so feel the loss of you

   your laughter

      your smile

         the silken caress of your hand

Yet . . .

   Through my tears

      I celebrate your re-emergence

somewhere . . .

            as the indomitable Soul you are,

Empowered once again

      to create, to move

         and to change things

In ways far beyond the ability

      of the life and body

         you have left behind

◆   ◆   ◆

Shera, they ask me, "How are you doing?"

With you gone, I feel as though I'm in an empty room with no doors, and no windows, no handles. Nothing to orient myself with. I know there are people around, friends come by. Nothing much has changed in the house, but in the middle of it all there is this empty space. The question transports me there in an instant.

How am I doing? In terms of what? Shera, I have nothing to compare it to, no idea what I should be expecting. I am new at this. I have not done it before.

◆   ◆   ◆

I felt numb. Hollow. I never expected to be in this kind of emotional Neverland. It was as though I was in suspension. I never really had any expectation of what this moment would be like. I had never actually thought about it. There is no training for it. I was adrift in a sea of random thoughts and questions and emotions. Some of the emotions were entirely new and unfamiliar. They were almost physical. I was feeling my body in ways I had not known before; my stomach, my throat, my breathing.

Questions came up, but I had no one to ask for the answers. They just hung vaguely in my mind until something nudged them out of the way. So, when I was asked, "How are you doing?" what was I to say? There needs to be something more than, "I don't know."

I was in a whole new world.

THE DEATH CERTIFICATE

So now we were at this place. All of our positive intention, all of our energy and joint efforts had finally been reduced to the piece of paper I was holding in my hands, "A Notice of Death." Another "new now."

Even as I watched my hand filling out the form, there was a part of me screaming inside, protesting, "This is not happening!"

It was as though by inscribing Shera's name on the document, I was making it happen. And yet I continued. I was also aware of a growing calm, a kind of acceptance, in completing the form. I could feel it helping me release all the pent-up ongoing efforts and single-minded intention I had carried for the past days and weeks. As my pen made it way over the form, it was drawing a line across the endless hope against hope that had driven me for years.

A weight I'd been unaware of was lifted from my shoulders.

It was done.

◆ ◆ ◆

On the outside things continued—food, drink, bathroom . . . the usual, although if the truth be told, I didn't feel hungry and I forgot to drink. The things I could see, I could deal with if I had to, even though in those days I didn't care too much about what I was looking at; an unmade bed, cluttered counters, the unusual disorder in the house. On the outside, what I could see was manageable. It's what I couldn't see that was unsettling and confusing. It raised questions. I needed to understand more. There was more here I needed to know.

❖ I was discovering the things I had taken for granted. Over our time together, my life had found form and direction based on the reference point of Shera's presence. Her passion and projects had become a part of my life. With the certainty of that reference point, my work, my decisions, and my activities had all gained context, purpose, and momentum.

Now that reference point had been removed, and part of me felt as though I was a ship at sea that, having lost its compass, found itself vaguely off-course, unfocussed, and moved by unseen currents.

My days were a completely new experience to me. It was hard to recognize what was important. Routines that had been carved into the morning hours and the evening hours had just evaporated. Pills and supplements that had been counted weekly and delivered daily for years, morning and evening, meant nothing now. They sat in the usual places, lined up in the bathroom, organized in the kitchen, untouched, suddenly irrelevant.

After all, how does one register an *absence;* emptiness? It is strange. Shera was gone. Okay. That had happened before. Every day for all the years we were together there were moments, hours, days, or even longer when we were apart; when I couldn't see her or didn't know where she was. When she was effectively "gone."

But this was different.

Until now, whenever we were separated, I had an unconscious assumption, a "knowing," that it was only a matter of time, a few moments or hours, before she'd be back and we'd be together again. Now, once again, we were separated. Shera was no longer here. This time, I *knew* she was not coming back. Yet the old assumption that she would return was still there. It was subliminal. It operated independently of my mind. It was energetic. Visceral.

In those early days of Shera's departure, it was this subliminal assumption of an inevitable reunion that was confounded. At random moments it continued to surface in the new reality of this reshaped world I was in. Sure, I may have "known" a reunion would not happen, but there were so many other levels outside of my mind that simply hadn't gotten that message yet.

I didn't *understand* what had changed. That's what made it seem so unreal. Again and again, I could feel it. I had removed its charge, unplugged the until-now-realistic expectation of Shera returning home, and replaced it with . . . what exactly? Nothing? a void? I was left wondering where she had gone. I wanted to know where Shera was.

❖ *That's* where the pain came up. It was not my refusal to accept that Shera was gone. After all, I worked to ease her departure, so that really hadn't been the issue. It was my having to deny all possibility *that she would return*; having to disavow the subliminal well-proven expectation—and hope—that she might "bounce back."

How was I supposed to integrate the loss of the comfort that expectation had once given me?

THREE PHASES OF LOSS

In looking back over this time, I recognize that before I would be able to fully appreciate what "losing" Shera meant, and before her departure would become "real," I would go through three levels of loss. Only then would I be able to begin integrating the implications of what I had just gone through.

THE FIRST PHASE OF LOSS: THE PASSING

The days of the vigil leading up to Shera's final departure were like a dream. They were surrealistic. Time had lost all meaning. The rest of the world disappeared. We were suspended in a cocoon enveloped in the love of those who were part of the vigil. The illusion was profound: Time, space, and distance lost all meaning. Hours of the day passed unnoticed. Morning moved to afternoon and on to evening seamlessly. Distance vanished as families in North America, South America, and Hawaii came together at Shera's bedside. At one point I was in the laundry room folding towels and sheets, and found myself wondering what to make them for breakfast when they came down in the morning!

❖ In this emotionally charged time, I had an advantage that many waiting in anticipation of the passing of a loved one simply do not have. I *knew* Shera was leaving within days, and had those days to prepare myself for the ultimate moment. That is why Shera's passing was not as traumatic as it otherwise might have been. I gave thanks for this. Anyone losing a loved one unexpectedly in an accident, or any sudden death, is denied this gift.

Moreover, Shera had *decided* to leave. Knowing her departure was imminent and that she had chosen to accept it, made it easy and natural for me to shift away from "saving her." I resolved instead to "escort" her to the "Door," as I called it, as best I could. I wanted her to know that she was safe and that everything was okay, that she was not alone, and that she was loved. I believe that is why, after seven tranquil days, when she ultimately passed on so painlessly and easily, the first emotion I had, oddly enough, was the feeling of success.

I did not know at the time that this was just the first phase of a journey I had just begun.

THE SECOND PHASE OF LOSS: BUSY-NESS

The next phase of loss began immediately after Shera's departure. It started with washing her body and sending her body to the funeral home. It continued to unfold for the following couple of weeks. In spite of the distractions and busy-ness being entirely focussed on what had happened, paradoxically, I found many of things needing to be done were actually distancing me from the *experience* of it.

In a way this phase can be seen by many as a blessing. It offers things to do, things to fill the void. "Do something" has long been a standard piece of advice to help people get through challenging times. It distracts them from their emotion. It acclimatizes them gradually. In my case, it helped orient me to the reality of what had just taken place.

I moved into the second phase the morning after Bob and Marianne drove off with Shera's body, when I woke up disoriented, feeling the emotional impact of being in my home without my beloved. Finding things that needed to be done gave me a kind of lifeline leading me to some sense of order.

The first thing I needed to do was to let people know what had happened. So many dear friends had been monitoring Shera's health for the past few years. Up until now we had all had gotten in the habit of celebrating Shera's resilience, and holding the expectation that she would bounce back from whatever life challenge she was facing. This time it was different.

I drafted a notice, a portion of which is quoted at the opening of Chapter 2, and sent it out to all the people I could think of who loved Shera or regarded her as a friend.

CELEBRATION OF LIFE

I had been in contact with Spar one or two times a day for the first weeks after Shera left. As we shared our feelings and the emotional impact of all that was happening, we turned inevitably to discussing what would happen next. We agreed that a funeral was not an option and decided to have a celebration of life within a week of Shera's passing.

However, in May 2020, the COVID-19 pandemic was dominating the news. Government-imposed mandates and travel quarantines were making air travel almost impossible for most people. Yet as it turned out, the constraints of the COVID-19 restrictions and limitations became a blessing.

Spar and I had been very pleased with the Zoom vigil that we had just had for Shera's passing. It had been very easy and effective. Although I had intended the vigil to host just Shera's immediate families, word had been passed on to other close friends, and by day three up to forty or fifty people had joined us in the vigil.

At that point, for Shera's sake and the intimacy I felt the moment deserved, I decided the call would be limited to family members for whatever time remained. (I knew having the faces of her family she cherished right beside her would give her the greatest comfort.)

Nevertheless, I was gratified to hear several people who had joined the call comment on how powerful the vigil had been for them, and how honoured they felt being able to be witness so intimately the days leading to Shera's departure. One friend shared that it had been profoundly healing for him. In his case, he had been unable to be with his father in India when he passed away. Seeing me with Shera, waiting with us, and feeling the love and the weight of the moment, he was able vicariously to find closure with his father's passing.

Because Zoom had handled the numbers that attended the vigil, we hoped it could handle a much larger celebration of life. So Spar upgraded his Zoom account to allow more participants and longer calls. We chose a date, put out the word and crossed our fingers.

Already sleep-deprived following the week-long vigil, Spar and Jib, Shera's second son, went long hours in the three to four days leading up to the event, working feverishly to complete video montages honouring their mother. I planned ways for people to participate.

Shera had dedicated much of her life to encouraging people to find their passion and express their creativity. So I suggested two things those we were inviting could do as a way of connecting with Shera and honouring her life's mission.

In the first, starting with the words "I heard the wind whispering . . . " they were to continue on writing for ten minutes, simply following their pen wherever their thoughts and emotions took them.

In the second, I asked them to "make a mark" on a page (as Shera would have said). In a similar way to the writing exercise, they were to continue on to whatever image or design would result.

Both exercises were something many of them had experienced at some time when they had been with Shera. Once completed they were to be sent to me.

It felt good to imagine that wherever Shera might be, she would be delighted to have so many people motivated in acts of creativity, expressing their love for her.

The celebration of life was successful beyond our expectations! One hundred and fifty people attended. At the start of the call, each of Shera's three sons and I spoke briefly. Then the videos Spar and Jib had created were shared. Afterward, we opened the call up to the participants. We invited them to share their experiences and impressions of Shera, and particularly how she had touched their lives. Then we sat back and listened as all the stories unfolded—*over the next five and a half hours!* I was profoundly impacted by this event. Certainly, the love and intimate sharing was hugely satisfying to witness.

❖ More than that, however, in the hours of storytelling I heard delightful things about Shera *I had not known*! All those times I mentioned earlier when Shera was away from me—when she was working in the garden with someone, or walking with a friend, sharing an activity, or out on an errand . . . I had never given any of it any thought. It was what it was.

However, in the Zoom calls, in story after story, I heard about how something Shera did or said—or just the way she was—had transformed someone, or had been a gift, and had changed someone's life for the better. Even though I had loved and lived with this woman for thirty-four years, these accounts opened up a whole new sense in me of who she truly was.

I became aware of her in a completely unexpected way. With this new perspective, I gained a glimpse of how Shera had been with *other* people. Through these stories I became aware for the first time that she had been a gift to many people beyond anything I had known or could imagine. It opened a whole new dimension for me of who Shera was, and what her unique gift was. Something I had not really thought of before.

Then I realized I was also learning what her *purpose* was for being here.

Without that call I might never have seen the *magnitude* of the woman I had shared my life with for so many years.

THE FINAL GOODBYE

The next thing to "do" after all the intensity leading up to the celebration of life was to arrange for my sweetheart's body's final journey. To the crematorium. Once again, I felt my ignorance. For example, where in one's day-to-day life does one learn about cremation? All I knew was that the body burns. Cremation was Shera's choice. Beyond that I knew nothing.

I called Christine, the funeral home director, to ask about the cremation process. She was very generous and transparent in describing it all. Then she got to the point where she said, "Then they'll gather all the ashes and transfer them to a box." My mind immediately recoiled with a spontaneous thought: "But Shera's always been *outside* the box . . . I don't want her ashes going into a box."

Christine then explained how the ashes were processed and added, more to herself, "I don't think there are many people who want to know this."

I *did* want to know this. I felt a personal responsibility for Shera's body and it was important to me that it be treated personally, with respect, and not as part of a generic "process." I did not want "Shera" processed. I also realized I wanted to be involved as much as possible.

She told me I would meet the hearse at the ferry terminal, and once on the other side, I'd drive behind them to the crematorium.

As it turned out that is not the way it happened.

Although by nature I tend to go along easily with others' expectations, in this case a voice inside me said, "This has to be done properly. There is no second chance."

What was expected by others was not as important as doing what I felt was "right" by Shera. I was somewhat bemused to realize what was "right" in this case was entirely mine to determine. I started exploring possible options with Christine.

In the end, *every* person I dealt with—Christine, Helen, who helped with the casket, and Steve and Brian at the crematorium— were all sensitive, supportive, and willing to meet my every wish. I felt seen and heard—and I was very grateful. In the end, I was able to carry out every aspect of the cremation. Although I had no inkling of it at the start of my call with Christine, this was exactly what I wanted.

Despite the rules and regulations that could have been invoked to prevent my participation, they were simply never mentioned. Nothing really was done in the process that I didn't do myself. I felt so well received.

On the day, Ollie, a young friend, accompanied me. He had been a volunteer and worked a couple of times with Shera and me. We had enjoyed each other immensely. Shortly after receiving notice of Shera's passing, Ollie had called me to offer his support and had come to stay with me for a couple of weeks.

❖ He was an unforeseen gift, and his help and bright attentiveness eased many of the challenges I was facing. Having someone with me over this time was profoundly comforting.

By the time we went to collect the cardboard casket with Shera's body from where it was being held, I had over a hundred messages of love and acknowledgment for Shera in the writings and artwork that I had asked friends to send to me. Olliie and I had compiled them and printed them the night before. I balled each of them up and nestled them all around Shera's body.

Then we put the casket in the back of my small pickup truck for the drive, first to the ferry, and then on to the crematorium.

When we arrived, I transferred the casket to a gurney and rolled it to the front of the furnace, or "retort." Once there, I put some fragrant purple lilacs on it from a bush in Shera's garden. It had burst into bloom the week she left. Using coloured markers, I set about changing the dreariness of the cardboard. At Spar's request, I wrote the words "Return to Sender!" across the top of the box and added some hearts and "Thank yous."

Then, under the guidance of the two men who normally would have performed the cremation, I slid the cardboard casket into the retort, essentially a large kiln, and pushed the buttons that closed the door. Then I pushed another button that fired up the secondary chamber and after a few moments, put the retort into full fire.

Shera's body, the last physical testament of her journey here with us, was now being transformed and purified in the flames that would burn away any remaining energy which might impede her Soul's onward journey. The flames would also carry the messages of the love and gratitude that went into the fire with her body—tokens of the love and blessing of the people she cared for and loved—for the flames to carry to her wherever she was.

It was immensely gratifying for me to have been able to release Shera's body to its final transformation, just as I had released her Soul to its new adventure.

Then I went out into the forest nearby to be with my thoughts. In the dappled light of the bright sun beaming through the trees, I sat on the thick moss covering the forest floor. The setting was exquisite! I felt deeply connected with everything around me. Bright new spring growth on the fir trees, lush mosses, and new ferns. Four ravens were there to greet me. One stayed with me after the others left, watching me from its perch on the top of the tree beside me. He cawed gently to me for half an hour, at times "gifting" me with bits of lichen and moss he dropped from his perch. Quite remarkable! Particularly because Raven is my power animal.

After a further half hour of soaking in the beauty of the woods, I was back at the crematorium to learn the cremation had taken less time than expected and was complete.

I was permitted, in spite of regulations, to gather Shera's body's ashes myself. Before leaving home, I had been looking without success for something for that purpose, when I stumbled across a great ceramic bowl I had not seen for over three years. It was the perfect bowl! She had made it herself fifty years before, to celebrate her role as mother in the way she had once dreamed it would be. On the lid her fingers had fashioned an intimate grouping of figures. The larger one representing her was lying in the centre. Two smaller figures, the sons she had hoped to raise, reclined against it, while another small figure, nestled up behind it, represented a third son, the firstborn child she had to adopt out at birth.

Driving home with the bowl and its sacred load in the back of the vehicle, I marvelled at how beautifully the day had unfolded. I felt blessed and grateful to have played such a significant part in this final purification and release of Shera's body. Because the idea of cremation had always been a bit unsettling for me, really had not known how I would handle the finality of it. Yet I was surprised and pleased at how remarkably positive and buoyant I had been throughout the whole day.

What needed to be done had been done. I felt complete.

That was when I moved into the Third Phase of Loss.

◆　　◆　　◆

There comes a time after the first days following a loved one's passing when immediate support has dropped off and the survivor is left alone to cope with the reality of their loss. This is a time when grieving can become intense, and there is little others can do to help.

There are intimate reminders every day of the absence of the loved one. Familiar routines and expectations can become awkward and uncomfortable. Everything and every event is a potential trigger.

Understanding this may offer insights that will serve you whether you are expecting to lose someone, have experienced loss yourself, or simply want to better understand what others who have lost a loved one may be going through.

CHAPTER 4

The Minefield

WHAT IS THIS SHADOW?

What is this shadow
    lurking here
       inside me
           somewhere in my body
Waiting
    for a quiet moment
       when I am alone,
          open and unfocussed?
What is this furtive apprehension
    that threatens to distract me
Drawing my attention
    into the disquiet
       that is hiding in the hole
         in my stomach?

A vague knot rising up

unexpected

unbidden

insistent

A thread tied to unexpected thoughts

out of place

unwanted

Like a magnet

drawing shadows of memories

to the threshold

of my conscious mind

This subtle insistence

will turn my focus

to this gnawing discomfort

To make me notice

give it place

and make it real

And if I give in

If I embrace this formless ache

this seed of some dark emotion

It can only grow

to bear a fruit

that causes pain.

It is a placeholder for grief

over and over

again and again

I feel its siren call

pulling me

And every time

again and again

I let it go unheeded.

I must let it go

It can only become

a smudge

. . . or more . . .

on the clear window

Opening to the vision I am creating now

of the new future

unfolding before me

That Shera wants for me . . .

Is building with me . . . .

◆　　◆　　◆

This sense of gratitude and appreciation stayed with me all the way home from the crematorium. When I got home, I lifted the heavy ceramic bowl with its precious cargo into my arms. As I turned from the truck, I was welcomed by the billowing expanse of red and pink flowers before me, radiant in the brilliant mid-afternoon sunshine. The camellia and rhododendrons flanking the front porch had only come into blossom in the few days since her passing. I had not yet seen them because I had largely remained inside for weeks. The beauty of the moment took my breath away, and I paused for a moment to soak in the wonder of it. Flushed and grateful, I turned to the porch and stepped through the front door.

THE THIRD PHASE OF LOSS: THE MINEFIELD

In an instant, everything imploded. The beauty and brightness evaporated, and the day went cold. Standing alone in the front hall, I felt like the walls were caving in on me.

I was carrying Shera's *ashes* in my arms. That was *not* how it was supposed to be! Shera was supposed to be *on* my arm! We had so many things we had yet to do. A return to our families in Peru. A trip to Africa. This, what was happening, was so wrong. I felt deeply the inescapable finality of it.

And I dissolved into tears, sobbing.

I sat several minutes in the living room sobbing, the bowl still in my lap. This was my initiation into the feelings of loss, powerlessness, and sadness that, looking back, I should have expected right from the beginning.

◆　◆　◆

It had taken this long to have the feeling of grief. I had expected it so much earlier. Even as I had seen myself coping "remarkably well," I had wondered about it. It was a strangely contradictory state to be, having just "lost" the one I love. Several things had contributed.

❖ Perhaps it was because, although the healing sessions had been committed to Shera's recovery, I had unconsciously been preparing myself for another possibility.

❖ Perhaps it was because when Shera decided to leave, I totally committed myself to *supporting* her in her decision. Ironically, this shift of focus had given my experience of Shera's passing the veneer of "achievement" instead of loss.

Perhaps it was because right from the start I had been spared any pretext for anger or frustration, thanks first to the exceptional support and assistance I received from everyone I encountered. Everything had unfolded incredibly smoothly.

Perhaps it was because after she left, I had encountered no "triggers," nothing that might have set me off. The things that needed to be "done" occupied my full attention.

However, from long before Shera passed and for pretty much the whole time since, I had been sleep-deprived. My resilience was low. I had also taken very little time to reflect on the implications of what had happened, and internalize the reality of my loss. In spite of appearances, I was emotionally fragile.

In retrospect, I believe the combination of all these elements had kept me from directly facing the implications of Shera's leaving. I also believe, as I mentioned before, that distraction is the *purpose* of the Second Phase of Loss. Busy-ness delayed my full immersion into the reality of what I had lost and what it would mean. Much of what I wanted to do was unconventional. I was directing the energy I had to making sure those tasks stayed on track.

❖ In addition, from the beginning my attention had been caught up in my drive to understand what had happened. I was writing and recording my endless thoughts and questions. It was effectively another kind of "busy-ness" that had acted as a buffer, shielding me from my feelings.

In that context, my arrival home from the crematorium marked the completion of the "doing" that had distracted me. I'd had a quiet and relaxing day. My mind had been at rest. However, arriving home set me squarely on the threshold of a new Reality beyond planning and expectation, which I could no longer deny. When I stepped through the doorway into my house, something dormant inside suddenly snapped awake with the undiluted realization that Shera was, indeed, *gone!*

◆　◆　◆

Shera, it feels like there is something subtle, hanging like a shadow, a vague threat somewhere between the unconscious and the conscious. It's like I want to avoid some pain, but I still need to understand what this is about. If I don't name it, or understand what it is, it will just keep pushing and pushing. I have been feeling this knot in my heart, in my stomach, and I'm torn between allowing it to be what it is because it is so real, or being without it and feeling . . . what? Nothing? No. I don't want it to become nothing, I just want it to be present without any discomfort. Having your energy with me without the pain coming in at some point. I don't ever want it to go away.

TRIGGERS

What was so hard was feeling Shera's presence. She was so totally here—everything in this place, every item I saw was hers or sparked a memory of her. It seemed every reflex I had was a habit built over years for her care and the recovery of her strength and the regaining of an active life for her—for us—for our future together.

And yet I could not touch her. I could not see her. Shera . . . was . . . not . . . here. It was so hard to comprehend how such a hugely vital presence and source of joy to so many people could vanish, to become as ephemeral as a dream.

At that time, when the centre of my life, the fabric and glue that had given shape and purpose to my life had just disappeared, the words "pull yourself together" took on new significance. It was no longer a metaphor. So there was a kind of automatic imperative to "manage." It was a conscious act on my part to keep my emotions from overwhelming whatever it was that might come next.

I would not let these reflexive thoughts become a loop sucking me into who knows where.

Does this mean I was suppressing my feelings? Not really. For a while initially, I was able to just keep taking the steps that were before me to take, and ride the wave of emotions that would come over me at times.

❖ At times when I had feelings of frustration, confusion, or disorientation I did not think of sharing them much with friends. Instead, from early on, and more so as days and weeks progressed, I found I was able to release my feelings into letters and poems I was writing almost daily, and even in conversations I continued to have with Shera, such as those I have shared at the beginnings of these chapters. I think perhaps this may have been what kept the intimacy alive between us that made possible what was to come.

It was, in a sense, a continuation of a dynamic that began long before Shera left, in which conversation had established a link between us. In spite of the challenges she faced following her stroke, Shera wouldn't hesitate to initiate a conversation with friends or launch forth with things she wanted to say. Whenever she "hit a wall" and the words she wanted to say had not lined up in the right way or evaded her completely, as often as not I would spontaneously pick up where she faltered, completing the comment she had intended to say. After all, I had been with her for decades and literally beside her almost 100 percent of the time in the past three years. I knew her stories and the rhythm of her thoughts.

It is so poignant to look now at the photos of Shera taken through the last six months of her life. They show her painting, playing, lifting tiny weights. (See page 39) Just three months before, Shera was still "challenging" young friends who visited or volunteered here to arm wrestle! She would try with all the strength in her, a radiant smile on her face. It was not a competition, it was for the play . . . the connection.

SECOND GUESSING

There were so many things I might have done differently, so many other therapies I might have found, signs that I might have noticed.

Shera, you know I really did try my best. Reading, researching online, checking this against that, and trying to intuit my way through the pharma-bias and censorship that always weighted information against proven naturopathic treatments and cures, invariably warning against dire consequences and risks if I should ever dare to stray away from the pharmaceutical options. It was hours a day mixing the potions and sorting the pills, and administering all the bits and pieces at the right times through the day. This pill not too soon after that pill. This supplement a half hour before meals, and those two hours afterward. We quietly endured it all. We both believed and carried on.

I recognize now, Shera, how earnestly, how naively I was caring for you. So many things! Doing my best . . . was I doing my best? Every day I was discovering profound new depths of my ignorance. Endlessly I sought to find ways to skirt around it, to alleviate it. I discovered a never-ending flood of amazing "proven cures" for cancer. That one, so promising, could not be considered because of Shera's blood pressure. This one we'd have to forget about because she was on a blood thinner. So often feeling disappointed for having to settle for something less.

I thank you my dear for trying so hard, for being so at peace with what was happening, for wherever we ended up in this bushwhacking search for the way that would bring you back to health. I thank you for never failing to believe that healing was possible, that a turnaround could occur. That a miracle could happen.

There were so many assurances by experts and proponents of so many "systems" and products. The odds looked so good, even as we understood, and accepted, that we could not know for sure what the outcome would be.

I am moved to tears, even today, by your unwavering trust in me. I can still marvel at how readily you would take "ownership" of whatever therapies and treatments I was recommending to you. You, like I, had such faith that, in the chaos of so many choices and changes, we would find the key to turn things around. Your commitment . . . your faith in me . . . was so apparent in the way you embraced what I suggested as the next best thing that would bring you back.

When I think of your grace and the courage of your belief that I was doing the best I could for you, I feel a twinge of discomfort. (Surely I could have done better.) Even though we both could see only recovery, Shera, your life was in the balance. Yet you never challenged me or argued. You had such faith, such confidence in me. I never saw doubt, and felt no hint of blame. Still . . . I guess . . . what other options did we have?

IF ONLY

Finding myself here in the aftermath of our failed effort to turn this decline around, there are so many questions that compete at times for my attention.

Perhaps if I had not been in such a bubble of positivity the whole time, I would have upgraded my assessment of her state and properly registered the persistent downward trajectory of her condition. Instead, like Shera herself, I was more focussed on her daily "breakthroughs" and accomplishments, however tiny they may have been: her smiles, the moments of playfulness, the jokes. It was later in viewing video clips that I could see clearly through her buoyant style how terribly challenged her communication had become.

Perhaps if I had fully registered the degree of loss of function she had suffered and how increasingly dependent she was on me, maybe something more could have been done.

Perhaps if I had seen the growing "shadow," I would have been more diligent in finding other things we could have tried, and worked harder to ensure we were doing all we could.

Perhaps if I had not been so intent on seeing good news, we would have monitored changes differently, and insisted that the doctors did as well.

Perhaps if I would have challenged what in retrospect was an obvious—and critical—misdiagnosis that failed to recognize the return of the cancer, it wouldn't have had a free run for ten months.

Perhaps if we hadn't decided to cure her from the cancer ourselves.

Perhaps if Shera and I not been so single-mindedly confident that she would recover from this just like she had recovered from every other challenge.

I know all of these doubts mean nothing now, and can only pull me down. I try not to give them any energy.

WORDS FAIL

❖ Creativity, whether expressed in words, paintings, or drawings, can be an important part of healing. It offers a way to release pain, integrate loss, and grow from trauma. Words or works of art can become steps to climb out of the "depths of despair." In times of crisis Shera always turned to drawings and art.

I am looking for my words. There are so many feelings and thoughts that pop up, unbidden, vying for my attention. When I am charged with emotions I cannot identify, they can be unrelenting and insistent, like a child in the store begging and tugging at me. Repetitious. Looking for attention, wanting *expression*.

It is so strange to feel emotions and not be able to identify them . . . or the words to describe them. There's so much more to my tears than sadness. "Loss" loses meaning. There is more depth than that. There is a rich, unidentifiable reflective quality to what I am feeling . . . a subtlety that dances on the edge of sadness, but with more consciousness to it.

I mourn the poverty of the language. English has abandoned me.

I have been so grateful to have had my journals and my ongoing "conversations" with Shera. I have had others at home here willing to sit every day, encouraging my attempts to share my thoughts and feelings, helping me to understand.

THERE ARE NO MISTAKES

In these weeks as I made my way through my "minefield," I would find myself at various times spontaneously in regret or longing; holding random thoughts of protest or denial:

"What if . . .?"

"If only . . ."

"You deserved better!"

❖ Then I would remind myself that such thoughts are totally irrelevant. They lead nowhere. They accomplish nothing positive. They can only serve to perpetuate the pain and accentuate the grief, with no possibility of changing the situation.

I felt at times, with regard to preventing these thoughts and regrets from gaining momentum it was like I was training a child to walk:

"No, no. Don't go there!"

"You'll fall down."

"Be careful!"

"Don't touch that!"

"You'll hurt yourself."

Shera, there are no mistakes. That's what we said every day for months.

It cannot be undone. It is what it is. You have passed.

Yet such thoughts persist. What drives them? It is easy to say it is the wounded child inside wanting something it cannot have and trying to resist whomever it is that is saying "No." Or it could be the ego, believing in its perpetually self-absorbed way, that it can change things over which it has no influence whatsoever. I feel it protesting now:

"Yes, but I *should* be able to change it."

"It *should* be different than it is."

"You should still be here!"

Oh my! When I am not caught up in the heat of such thoughts, the contradictions of such thinking immediately become evident. They are breathtaking. "You 'should' be here?" What exactly does that mean?

You *should* be back in a body that is beyond worn out? You *should* be here, continuing to suffer the pain, discomfort, and indignities of being utterly dependent on others? You *should* be back in your body striving for recovery. Recovery? Really? Recovery of what? The ability to stand? To walk? The ability to feed yourself and go to the bathroom on your own? The ability to continue *striving?* No my dear! You deserve so much better than crawling on and on indefinitely, in the hope of recovering some limited capability in some area.

What irony! All these months—years?—working with you, intent, dedicated to recovering your health, functionality, and independence so you could regain your life.

❖ And now I am celebrating your freedom. Now at last you are free from struggle. Free from the pain and indignities of a body that was well and truly finished. You are free and flying in another world. *That* is where you *should* be! How could I wish anything less for you?

SHADOWS

For months after Shera passed, I had quietly chosen not to think much about her gallery. It had been a major focus of Shera's passion, a monument to her accomplishment as an artist. It is the embodiment of the future she dreamed of. Ultimately, it had become her final accomplishment. For me, being in the gallery stirred up too many thoughts and emotions. I was uncomfortable there. It was emotionally painful to see the once-vibrant space in such disarray, so I had been avoiding it. It embodied Shera's dreams of fulfilment and recognition as an artist at the apex of her career, now forever ended.

Three years earlier, when I was walking with her in the hospital garden after a particularly harrowing crisis had concluded favourably, I heard myself asking something I had never asked before: "Shera, how are you doing with all of this?"

Tears came to her eyes. First, she said, "I wonder if I will ever see my three sons together again." She had been together with her three sons only once before, almost forty years earlier.

Then she added, "And I don't think I will ever see my gallery open."

It was the first time ever I heard her acknowledging her mortality.

Feeling the depth of her anguish, I coordinated the arrival of all three of her sons on her birthday two months later—a birthday surprise that succeeded beyond my wildest hopes. I managed to have each of them within two feet of her before she discovered them! It was a wonderful party that went on for five days.

One of her unasked wishes had been fulfilled.

However, four months later, as we were about to take up residence in our new home on Salt Spring, Shera suffered her stroke. *It happened only a month before she would have seen her gallery open.*

The stroke had been so devastating, doctors all doubted she would survive even the first three days. Fulfilment of her second wish had been denied.

However, Shera not only "survived" the stroke, she made miraculous strides in her recovery. And being who she was, the dream of seeing her gallery open became a major goal in that recovery. Two years after the stroke, Shera opened her Love of Colour studio/gallery—and hosted it for a full season! A major accomplishment. She not only saw her gallery opened, it was her best season ever.

A year later, she was gone.

For me, in the aftermath of her departure, her gallery had come to represent a mountain of unfulfilled potential. It literally embodied the inspiring expression of her creative genius, and the joy of her work . . . never-to-be-realized-again.

However, one summer day came when I had to admit to myself that I was not honouring the dedication Shera had to being in her gallery on the listed open days. It was long past time for it to be accepting visitors again.

I went into the gallery.

It was uncomfortable for me to look at the cot on which Shera had rested while waiting for visitors to arrive. Isolated on the floor, it strongly highlighted her physical absence now. Seeing the empty cot, since piled with odds and ends, blankets in disarray, her teddy bear toppled on its side, and the pillow still waiting to cradle her head . . . it was too much for me. I left.

Two days later, I was back in the gallery, this time in a completely different frame of mind. Something had broken the spell. It was easy. I moved as many paintings as I could into the storage bays, and arranged those left over into free-standing walk-around displays on the gallery floor. That done, I folded the blankets from the cot and moved the teddy bear onto a new perch above the card display. Then, finally, I folded Shera's cot and put it away. No problem. She would have approved. She would probably also have said, "A job won't go away until you get it at it."

On that weekend, the gallery was open and shining, proudly displaying the bright colours of joy in Shera's work—and the season's first visitors loved it!

Somewhere close by, I knew Shera was smiling.

I could not have anticipated the strange double life that was about to confuse my sense of my new "normal."

◆　　◆　　◆

The Second Lens—The Quest

Coincidences are part of everyone's experience. They are things noticed which normally escape our attention or bear mentioning only at special times such as marriages, birthdays, births, and deaths, as though we seek to elevate the importance of the event by attributing significance to happenstance.

It's understandable after a death, with the pain and yearning that accompanies loss, there might be a desire for *something* to happen which would give importance to a particular moment.

After all, whether it is expected or not, experiencing someone's final departure moves one to question . . . to *wonder.* How many opportunities are we given to expand our awareness? To work in the crucible that emotion offers, to forge a renewed sense of who we are in our lives and our relationships—indeed, a sense of what life is, and where it leads?

Through this second lens, I invite you to follow me on my journey as I encounter one bizarre event after another, which are clearly not "normal." How do they look to you? For me, these synchronous events gave rise to a quest driven by three questions:

"What just happened?"

"What is this all about?"

"Where did my sweetheart go?"

This lens shines another light into the Mystery which inevitably turns our attention, at least for a time, away from the mundane, and forces us to face the "unknowable."

We are playing our lives out in an amazing board game, unaware of the rules—or even the objectives—of the game. We create rules so the game will make sense to us. We calm our minds with an artificial order that shapes our beliefs and limits what we can see. Yet all the while we know we're not in control.

From time to time, hard on the heels of the Horseman of Death, the Trickster rides across the board. His lance drives holes though the shutters of the beliefs that frame and narrow our view of life, and for a brief moment we have a chance to see *beyond* our usual scope of vision.

Imagine what our lives could become if we didn't jump so quickly to patch the shutters.

CHAPTER 5

Cosmic Play

Thirty-four years, Shera. The time you were here beside me in the flesh. For all that time I took the continuity of your presence for granted. My experience of our being together, of our being in relationship, was tangible—real—and something we shared. Now with your passing, it has become something ephemeral; nothing more than a dream.

I don't even know what that means. The certainty of our relationship, and the dynamic of it; the essence of what we shared together is something that remains alive in me alone. Memories. No . . . it's more than that . . . it is hard to put my finger on it.

There is certainly evidence of you in photos and the things that you left behind. Your journals telling the stories of your life. That much at least is not just my imagination. And yet how do I conjure up or even put words to the magic, the energy, the mutuality of the two of us together, except in my imagination and my memories? Is that what is truly gone forever? Oh, my love!

◆　◆　◆

Before she left, I had hopefully asked Shera to let me know now and then, how she was doing . . . to let me know that she was okay. At the time I was thinking I might find a heart show up unexpectedly on occasion, because we had shared a pleasure in discovering heart-shaped rocks in our travels; or perhaps there would be an occasional eagle flying by. Shera had always considered the eagle to be her power animal.

I could never have imagined what was going to happen.

A LETTER FROM HEAVEN

I described in the previous chapter how, having just arrived home from the crematorium, I was sitting in the living room, the bowl carrying Shera's ashes in my lap, when I was suddenly struck with the reality of my loss. Instantly I was in tears. And with the tears came the pain. An ugly deep ache, a cesspool-like, cramping kind of feeling in my gut and body. An overwhelming convulsion of emotion of a sort I had never experienced before.

In desperation I realized, "I have to get out of this! I can't stay in this space!"

I opened my eyes. I had to do something! I looked at the bowl in front of me, "I have to put this some place."

Anything to distract me from this feeling of loss.

Looking around the room, my eyes settled on a small dresser by the windows to my right. With tears in my eyes, I walked over to it. The bowl was still in my arms. A stack of papers and magazines had accumulated on the top of the dresser, so I put the bowl on the floor and turned to clear the pile of papers away. I reached down, intending to gather them all, lifted them, and set them to the side.

When I looked back, I was surprised and more than a little confused to see a solitary paper still lying on the top of the dresser . . . a large 11" x 17" poster-size paper . . . face down. How could I have missed it? I picked it up and turned it over.

Suddenly, Shera was before me—*laughing!* with her hands raised joyfully to either side of her face, radiating delight from a photo on the paper in front of me. (See photo on page 8.) The shock and delight of seeing her radiating such joy lifted me completely out of the emotional chasm I had fallen into.

Just as suddenly, *I was laughing!* I had asked her to let me know how she was doing, and my heart leapt at the idea that this joyful image was her response.

I spent a moment or two indulging myself in what I have always felt was one of the best photos ever taken of her. Then I looked at the rest of the poster. I was instantly captivated by what I read:

> *I am I am I am*
>
> *Colour happens, Moves about me*
>
> *I burst beyond the frame that holds me.*
>
> *I want to step over my edge, explore new dimensions*
>
> *Connect with the greater Guidance, that moves and guides me.*
>
> *. . . I feel the life, its pulse, its beat.*
>
> *What it generates on subtle levels that speaks beyond the mind.*
>
> *Now I'm finished there's a feeling of delight*
>
> *A balance, a floating*
>
> *My inside has more freedom, it's been stretched, left its patterns*
>
> *And found NOW*
>
> *Juice moves to find its expression!*
>
> *My creative fountain overflows*

A letter from heaven? For this poem to show up in *this* moment, turning up in my hands at the very time I felt so lost, was extraordinary. I stood gazing at the poster, laughing at the delightful madness of it. I had just plunged completely into the suffocating embrace of grief for the first time; the first, full, searing realization that Shera was no longer with me . . . and just as suddenly Shera was right in front of me laughing! *"Telling"* me how she was doing—exactly what I had asked her for! The tears of grief still wet on my face had become tears of joy.

Even though she had written the poem over ten years earlier to celebrate the joy she felt in creating her art, in an instant, it had taken on completely new meaning.

I let myself savour the chaos of thoughts and emotions, wonder, and delight that coursed through me and I laughed again. Then I glanced back at the dresser.

I was surprised to see yet another piece of paper on the top of it. This one was tiny, the size of a large postage stamp. It was lying face down, in the *exact* centre of the dresser. I recognized it immediately as a card from our "Word Bowl" and wondered how this solitary card could have found its way from the bowl on the other side of the room, to lie *under* a stack of papers. Curious, I picked it up and turned it over.

On the card was the single word: *"Peace."* I felt an instant wave of warmth flood over me. In that instant, I *knew* Shera was still with me. I knew this was a way she had found to console me . . . with the perfect word to wish someone in distress.

It was a year later that I realized, in the captivating surprise of seeing Shera's beaming face on the poster, I had overlooked yet another element of the "message." Looking again, I noticed she was standing in front of one of her favourite large paintings . . . one she had painted as a celebration of our relationship.

WORD PLAY

It was in the evening, a couple of weeks after Shera had left. I was on a call with Magaly, our goddaughter in Peru. We had been checking in with each other every few days to share how we were doing. Sitting a few feet away from me, Ollie was at the dining table going through our Word Bowl. For some reason, he had decided to go through all of the eight hundred random words in the bowl just to see what they were. Remarkable!

Many years earlier, Shera had the idea of a word bowl, and together we had created all the cards that filled it. We would turn to the bowl at every opportunity to play with visiting friends and guests. It always brought laughter, and was one of Shera's favourite games to share with people.

After her stroke, the bowl took on a new significance. Determined to regain her ability to speak, Shera was never without a handful of word cards in her pocket. At every opportunity she would draw them out one at a time to read them, speak them and test whether she understood them.

In spite of the obvious challenge she faced, if we had visitors and the Word Bowl became the centre of activity, Shera was also involved, and putting everything she had into fully engaging in the creative play. Throughout her life, involvement had always been her personal recipe for joy and delight.

On the phone with Magaly, I asked, "What do you think the gift was that Shera brought to the world?"

And as I considered the question myself, I thought of the joyfulness in both Shera's manner and the bright colours of her paintings. Joy had been the beacon that had guided her through an unending succession of personal setbacks and life challenges. We had even decided to make "Joy" the brand of her gallery.

I said, "I think the gift Shera gave the world was joy."

Listening to us, Ollie, at the Word Bowl, started suddenly, the movement catching my eye. I watched as he leapt up from the table and walked toward me with a card in his outstretched hand, his eyes fixed on mine.

"Here is the card I just turned up when you said the word "joy" just now."

I looked at the word on the card he was holding out: "*Joy!*"

For an instant we exchanged glances, and then, together with Magaly in Peru, we broke into laughter, amazed. All of us thinking the unspoken thought: "Shera!"

We really felt her presence.

A little while later, after I had completed the call, I was still reflecting on what had happened when I noticed the brilliant colours transforming the evening sky. I turned to Ollie, who was still working at the bowl. "Ollie?" I mused whimsically, "Do you suppose Shera is painting the sunsets these days?"

Instantly Ollie started at the table and jumped to his feet again. He came over to me holding another card in front of him.

"When you said Shera's name I was turning this card up" I looked at the card:

"Joy". . . *again!* Almost eight hundred words in the bowl, yet the word "Joy" had surfaced twice on separate cards—each at the precise instant Shera's name was mentioned!

We broke into laughter again. This was hard to believe. It felt as though the living room had become electrified. *There were only two Joy cards in the bowl!*

A little while later, Ollie was back at the table, continuing with his task when he paused and leaned back. He was still thinking about what had just happened. He looked over at me as his hand automatically drew another card from the bowl.

"Unbelievable!" he said. "You know, when I picked the 'Joy' card the second time I felt like I was pushed back in my seat inside."

As I nodded my head and smiled, his gaze turned down to the card in his hand. His eyes instantly widened and he let out a loud laugh of disbelief, "Wha-a!?"

Once again, he got up and brought me the card, his hand stretched out before him. The word on the card? *"Inside!"* The very word he had just spoken.

We were both convinced Shera *was* playing with her Word Bowl again tonight! It felt wonderful. In the way it had all played out, I could feel her humour and playfulness and could almost sense her glee. *Three* times words had been drawn at *precisely* the instant we had uttered them.

It was the next morning, as I lay in bed musing on the remarkable synchronicities— *coincidences*—that I suddenly saw what had happened.

At the beginning of my call with Magaly, I had asked what the gift was that Shera had brought to the world. *From that instant on* it was as though Shera had joined our conversation, using her beloved Word Bowl. She had immediately set about giving us *her* answer to the question. What she brought to the world was "Joy . . . Joy inside."

I had to laugh. I am a word person, and very verbal. Shera had literally spelled out her answer for me, so to speak, *word by word!*

In my journal that night I said, "This experience tonight has resolved whatever doubts I had about whether Shera was still here with me."

❖ For the first time, I felt I was being encouraged to let go of the sadness that had touched me at times when I saw things reminding me that she is gone. "I may not see her, but she is not gone. Shera, through her Word Bowl was reassuring me she never left me—*and* she was letting me know what she wanted for me: "Joy. Joy inside."

I knew wherever she was she had to be smiling.

SILENCING A SHADOW VOICE

Whenever I noticed a coincidence or synchronistic event, there was always a shadow voice inside, instantly ready to challenge whatever I might be taking as a possible "message" from Shera. The voice is a product of the years I spent in university studying science. I recognize it in my desire to default to "objectivity" where possible. I accepted some things may just be my imagination, or even delusory thinking. Possibly denial. Perhaps just another face of grief.

But these Joy cards? Not so easy to dismiss. What are the odds of drawing each of those words at *precisely* the time they were relevant, simply by chance? In addition, what other word could have been a more appropriate answer to the question we had asked? Yet there is another over-arching question: Why had Ollie decided to start the curious—*and tedious*—task of turning over *every* card in the Bowl at the *same* time Magaly and I started our conversation? In the twenty years we had the bowl, no one had ever *thought* of doing that!

TRANSFORMATION

In the evening a few days later, in spite of a feeling of reluctance, I went out to join a sunset drumming circle being hosted by friends on a nearby beach. With Shera's passing, I had not been much into parties, and I was not feeling much like socializing. On top of that, I have always been self-conscious about what I considered my limits as a drummer.

Shera loved such gatherings, especially drum circles. I even had her hand drum and two beautiful conga drums she had had built over fifty years ago. Then a thought dropped into my head: "If Shera were here, she would never miss an evening like this."

I decided to go.

In spite of myself, I ended up thoroughly enjoying the evening—and actually managed some almost-rhythms on the drums. I came home feeling lighter and refreshed and slept well.

The next morning, while reflecting on the evening, my attention turned to the word bowl. A thought came to me. "I wonder if Shera might have a comment about it?"

I reached into the bottom of the bowl and drew three word cards: Creativity, Joy, and Transformation.

Look at that! "Joy" again!

Transformation was Shera's prime intention in the creative healing work she did with others. From the beginning of our relationship "transformation" had also been her intention for me. She wanted me to release my creative expression and play more! This morning it seemed I was getting an encouraging reminder!

Then, later in the day I received this text from her son Spar in Hawaii:

"I have these words that are going through my head over and over today . . . a question actually: 'Are you letting the transformational power of love have its way with you?'"

Totally non-plussed, once again I found my credulity being stretched by the 'coincidental' appropriateness of what Spar had said. It was perfect in the context of previous night.

Clearly what I was experiencing was not limited to the Word Bowl.

MORE WORD PLAY

A month later, on a Saturday I was talking to two young people, Tina and Marie Jean, about Ollie and the Joy cards. I decided to 'introduce' them to the card bowl by demonstrating what Ollie had been doing. As I told them the story. I reached into the bowl and drew a card, all the while maintaining eye contact with my two visitors. I picked a second one, automatically placing them in turn one beside the other on the table. Then, before drawing another card, I glanced down. It took a couple of seconds before I actually registered the words on the two cards I had just placed there.

The first card said "Meet," and the second said "Joy!"

The "introduction" had been completed—literally! And it had been made with Shera's characteristic touch of humour!

◆   ◆   ◆

When, in Shera's final week, I had whispered into her ear, my request to send signs letting me know how she was doing, I never dreamt that beyond "signs" I would be getting actual *messages*. Already on a quest to make sense of what had happened with Shera's passing, I now found myself with yet another question. Given the way we have been taught about "reality" and how the world around us works, how can these experiences possibly be real? To simply dismiss it all as "coincidence" seems to be a kind of intellectual cowardice.

It has been remarkable. In the creativity and the variety of ways these "messages" have come to me, it was easy for me to imagine Shera's humour at play. She had always considered me her "man of words" and so it was fitting and not just a little remarkable that so many her "messages" came literally as *written* messages. They have never stopped coming. The poster I had received when I got home from the crematorium was not the only "letter from Heaven" that I received.

ANOTHER MESSAGE FROM HEAVEN

About a week before Shera left, a couple had taken up residence into the basement suite. A couple of days after Shera had passed, I went downstairs to see how Shawn and Marilyn, the new tenants, were settling in. I commented on how I hoped they were okay with being literally surrounded by books. Over two thousand books occupied the shelves lining the walls. As luck would have it, both Shawn and Marilyn were book lovers and were quite delighted to have them.

Marilyn asked, "What about the two little books?"

I was a little confused. "What do you mean?"

She got up and crossed the room to retrieve two small spiral-bound volumes from a distant shelf. "These!"

"Oh!" I said, recognizing them instantly. "I haven't seen those for years. They were part of a book writing weekend we hosted almost twenty years ago. We each went home with our own book."

Then, picking one up, I said, "This is the one I made."

They listened politely as I read a short piece from my little book. Then, with barely a word of acknowledgment, Marilyn lifted Shera's book, which she was still holding in her hands, and pushed it forward for me to take. "Read this one!"

I felt strangely awkward for a moment, as though I was about to violate someone's privacy—it was Shera's book after all—before remembering the rules had just changed.

I opened the book at a random page. Shera had put a line of text on each page and added artwork around it. I read the line before me, and continued reading the following pages in succession, one after the other:

With love and conscious spirit I unfold into the world.

I am my teacher. I am my teacher. I am my teacher.

I've barely begun to tap my creativity.

It's time to be with nowhere to go and go with it.

Many Light Spirits dance around me in iridescent pastels guiding me constantly.

I'm part of a bigger team.

We were stunned. This long-forgotten book had been delivered into my hands, and it had opened on words that could be describing the experience of someone's arrival in Heaven. A message perfectly timed for the moment.

Messages and signs would not only be coming in words. They also came as animals. As one would expect, these were much more nuanced than something that comes in writing. Nevertheless, the inferences and contexts are clear.

Canada Geese

Two or three days after Shera's departure, I went out kayaking with Ollie. After an hour and a half, as we were about to come in, the thought suddenly came to me—despite the ebbing tide—to go under the bridge at the end of the estuary and into the marches beyond. Shera had once paddled there, and I had always been curious to check it out myself.

It was a sunny day, and we entered an exquisitely quiet world, meandering through the marsh grass to the end of the channel. We came upon two pairs of Canada Geese in the last pond. Although they showed some alarm at first, they calmed almost immediately. During the twenty to twenty-five minutes we shared space, I felt my mind going quiet.

Paddling back to the bridge, a thought popped into my mind that my partnership with Shera would continue. We'd still be a team. While I promoted her work on this side, as I had always done, she would "clear the way" for me from the other side. It felt obvious and natural to me. With that comforting thought in mind, I paddled home.

◆　　◆　　◆

Two weeks later, I was standing on the porch of the home Shera and I had sold before moving to Salt Spring. I had returned with Ollie to pick up some things we had left behind. It was an overcast day. We had stepped outside to join our host at his barbecue, drinks in hand.

On impulse, I proposed a toast to Shera, and at the instant we raised our glasses, there was a break in the clouds and the sun beamed onto our faces. Surprised, I looked at my friends, and the expressions on their faces left no doubt that they had noticed the synchronicity as well.

A couple of moments later, I noticed two Canada Geese flying in a straight line that would lead them to shore a few hundred yards to my right. However, at the instant I spotted them, they changed course. They were now flying on a beeline *right at me*. They landed in the water, directly in front of me, barely thirty feet away. Later, I learned that Luannah, the new owner, had also noticed them flying in. "I haven't seen them for some days now," she said. "I wondered what significance their arrival today might have."

❖ Taking that as a cue, I went online and searched for "spiritual significance of Canada Geese." I was amazed at what I read in the first page I clicked on:

> *Canada geese are known for their bravery, loyalty (It does not leave one of its kind behind), teamwork, confidence, protection, fellowship, communication, determination, and monogamy . . . When you see a goose, it's time for you to embark on your own journey of inner joy! You may be stagnant, or you may have tossed aside your own plans in order to live someone else's life and dreams. The goose is exhorting you to let go and follow it in flight.7*

The parallels with my life were appropriate and obvious. I had indeed effectively set myself to the side to support Shera in what were to be her last years. Since her passing I have recognized how Shera has been supporting *me* to start moving again, and exhorting me to "embark on [my] own journey *of inner joy*." *(There was that word again!)*

Turtles

During one enjoyable evening of writing with two friends, Elle and Jennifer, we finished by sharing with each other what we had written.

Clearly, at some level Shera was present with us in our thoughts, in the creativity and the readings.

As we were saying good night, Elle paused and turned to me. "Oh! Did you put the turtle on the ginger?"

I had no idea what she was talking about. So, she called me into the kitchen. There, perched on top of a piece of ginger in a basket by the stove, was a small yellow plastic turtle. I recalled noticing it there myself earlier in the day and had wondered where it had come from.

Elle declared, "I think Shera put it there."

I thought, "What an extraordinary thing to say!"

Elle had only been with us a couple of days and had not been fully initiated into the "coincidences" that had become part of our lives.

Despite all the phenomena I had been prepared to attribute to Shera so far, I could not recall anything being *moved* or lifted physically.

"Ollie probably put it there," I said.

Ollie, who had intended to be with me for a couple of weeks, had not yet left.

"No." Her reply was instantaneous. She explained, "It was Ollie who saw it first. He showed it to me and asked if I had put it there."

Later I checked with Ollie. "That's right," he said. "When I asked Elle, she just wanted to know if Shera was playful."

I was thoroughly bemused. Elle had never met Shera, but had certainly identified a key part of her character.

Then I suddenly remembered that Shera *loved* turtles. They had almost been the death of her!

A couple of weeks after narrowly surviving her congestive heart failure years earlier, Shera had gone to be with her son Spar in Hawaii. Another son, Robert, had flown in as well. They were on the beach together when they heard someone call out, "Turtles!" He was pointing to the sea. Shera was not going miss the chance to see them herself, and in the next instant she was in the water and swimming out into the open ocean.

Remarkably, she actually made it there. However, before she started to swim back, she suddenly became short of breath! Her heart couldn't handle the exertion. She would never have made it back to shore except that she had two angels with her in the form of her sons, both strong swimmers. They were able to tow her back to shore and lay her down on the beach where eventually she caught her breath again and recovered.

Of *course* Shera loved turtles! Shera had made several paintings of turtles. However, all of them were painted in dark greens and blues, not yellow. Then I remembered Shera had hung one in the living room and stepped back to show Elle.

My mouth dropped open. On the wall in front of us was a turtle painting rendered in dark greens and blues as I had described. However, below two of the blue and green turtles, brightly occupying the lower right quarter of the painting, was the third turtle—rendered in *yellow*! I looked at Elle in amazed confusion. All of Shera's other turtle paintings were painted as I had described, *entirely* in blues and greens.

After saying good night to Elle, I had an impulse to share what had happened with Spar, and went to the bedroom to call him. He picked up immediately.

"Wow! Amazing you called!" Spar said as soon as he picked up the phone, and before I had a chance to speak. "I have been thinking a lot about mom. For the first time in some time I had another good cry . . . missing her today."

Before I had a chance to share my story, he went on to share two more things. "I went to a memorial yesterday—for a friend named Elle."

How remarkable! The only person I ever met with that name was the Elle who brought the little yellow turtle to my attention.

Then Spar added, "I saw ten turtles swimming today."

Eagles

Shera always considered the eagle to be her animal totem, her power animal. She delighted in photos and videos of bald eagles, and in drawing and painting them. Among her personal treasures were two ceremonial eagle wing fans, feathers, talons, and even an eagle skull—gifts she had harvested from a dead eagle she came across one day while walking in the forest.

Both she and many of her friends thought of her as an "eagle woman." This is one of the reasons I had assumed at the outset that if she were sending signs from the other side, they might come in some form of an eagle. So, after Shera passed, I was more than primed to notice any eagle-related happenings around me. Indeed, there have been many. Here are three examples:

The first incident was of an eagle nest built in the high branches of a fir tree down the channel from our home. It was huge, perhaps seven or eight feet across, and visible from our bedroom. It had been around a long time. In fact, a long-established holiday rental directly across the water from it was named The Eagles Nest, emphasizing the chance guests had to observe the activities of the eagle family as the chicks hatched, grew into fledglings, and finally took flight. It was something the neighbourhood looked forward to and followed with interest every year.

The year Shera chose to leave, the eagle pair did not take up residence in their nest for the first time ever. It remained empty the whole year. Then the following year, the nest fell out of the tree altogether. The end of an era. Like Shera, the eagles, too, had departed.

❖ ❖ ❖

When Shera passed, I sent out a notice of her passing to the young people who had been working with us at various times during the previous year as part of a volunteer program. They had all bonded with Shera and been a source of pleasure and vitality for her. It was a couple of days later I received the message from Ollie offering to help out for a couple of weeks through what were likely to be difficult days ahead. I was newly on my own and readily accepted.

Months later, he told me he had received my notice at a time he and his girlfriend had been going through a rough patch. She was planning on going to Calgary, but he was unsure whether that was what he wanted to do. My notice had given him a new option to consider. Always an outdoorsman, he went to a beachside park to be by himself to think it over.

"I was sitting there looking out to the water, wondering what I should do," he recounted months later, pausing briefly. "Then, suddenly, from somewhere behind me, an eagle appeared, flying almost directly above my left shoulder toward the ocean, where it circled once before landing on a log directly in front of me." He laughed, "I think Shera was trying to catch my attention, to help me make my decision!"

Ollie was a godsend to me. Aside from all the physical support in managing the property and gardens, he gave me the chance to verbalize and process all that I was going through, much of which was central to writing this book. Intending to come for three weeks, he continued on with me for five months.

◆　　◆　　◆

A year later, I was standing at the door of Shera's gallery talking with a friend. He had lost his wife in tragic circumstances just before meeting Shera and me a couple of years earlier. He was trying to decide where he could put some of his wife's ashes to honour them. As he spoke, I started to ask myself the same question about Shera's ashes.

Rising steeply immediately behind where he was standing, was a twenty-foot-high hill I had built to complement Shera's gallery. It was a main feature of the Japanese garden, which had now also become a memorial garden honouring her. I planned to have water flowing from the peak of the hill down a watercourse I had built through the garden and over four waterfalls into the pond below.

Starting from a small source pool at the top, the water would appear to flow out of a naturally sculpted heart-shaped rock, which had been a birthday present Shera had surprised me with years earlier.

Indicating the rock at the top of the hill, I said, "I think I would like to put some of Shera's ashes up there."

As I spoke, a flash of a shadow at our feet caught my eye. It had crossed the six or seven feet of open ground in a microsecond and was gone.

"Wow!" I said spontaneously. "That must have been a big bird."

Confused, my friend not having noticed anything, asked what I meant. When I told him about the shadow, he immediately stepped back so he could look up to the sun over the roof of the studio behind me.

Shading his eyes against the sun, he announced, "It's an eagle!"

Of course! I could only assume my plan had been approved!

PLAY

As you can imagine, I was fascinated and intrigued to be experiencing these "coincidences." While most of these events related to what was happening in the moment, there were also some that seemed to come out of the blue—for the fun of it, so to speak. I came to think of these as "*Sherandipitous* events" . . . Shera in her new cosmic playground, exercising her sense of humour.

Here's an example. It was a sunny Saturday in September around my birthday, four months after Shera's passing, and the gardening circle had been coming regularly for months. After lunch, a friend suddenly appeared from behind me carrying a large chocolate cake—a surprise birthday cake! It was quite impressive and ringed with (far too many!) candles, all burning brightly.

I was quite touched, and moving to stand in front of the cake, I expressed my thanks to everyone. Then I took a big in-breath in order to blow out the candles. Suddenly, without warning, *all* the candles—normal wax birthday candles—went out—*instantaneously*! It was as though they were on a switch. There was a moment of shocked silence and gasps as everyone registered what had happened. And then laughter. Someone called out, "I think Shera is helping you!" and we all laughed again.

Amazed, I checked to see if there was a wind. The air on this warm summer afternoon was completely still. No breeze at all. Imagine our surprise then, when, twenty seconds later, without warning, *all* the candles reignited again—*instantaneously*! Just like they were on a switch.

As I tell people this story, I am always thankful that Ollie was among those present. He recorded the whole amazing event on video with his cell phone.

When I reflected on this incident months later, I remembered that in all our time together Shera and I had never let a birthday go by without concocting some crazy way to surprise each other. This was my first birthday after she left. I had to laugh. The thought she might have managed this stunt "from the other side" put this birthday surprise in a league of its own.

WONDER

As you might imagine, I really didn't know what to make of the coincidences and synchronicities at the beginning. They were novel.

They were stimulating. I had no idea when they would happen, or what was coming next. I only knew they *were* occurring. In the beginning they seemed to be happening, in one way or other, almost daily. I could never have imagined how often and in how many remarkable ways they would occur. There was no warning of when they might come, or what form they would take, and there was no way of denying them when they happened.

❖ One exciting realization is that such amazing events and synchronicities could be happening around us all the time. I believe that is true. We have simply lost the ability to notice. We have lost *wonder*.

As these coincidences continued to occur, I wanted to better understand what was happening. I could not just dismiss them as accidental. Again and again, these events were strikingly appropriate and relevant to the moment in which they occurred. Over and over again, they were consistent with the values and priorities that Shera had held. That was how I came to believe that they had to be linked with Shera.

❖ In any case, I learned to share the stories without apology. After all, what was happening *had* happened. How could these synchronies be random events? There were so many questions. I found myself wondering if there could be *intention* in everything that happens. If so, then *whose* intention is it? Was it indeed Shera who was behind these phenomena? Or something bigger? Who was to say? Was it I, myself, creating them? Was it some Trickster, an angel, some Higher Power? I felt somewhere in all of these experiences, was the key to unlock the answers I was seeking.

I began to wonder, "How is this possible?"

"Is this something that only happens with me?"

"How many others have had similar experiences?"

It made me realize how important it is for people who have experiences like this to share those experiences, at least with friends and family. Then, perhaps others like me wouldn't find themselves alone, trying to understand what to make of the things they are experiencing. Imagine how that would expand the awareness in all of us of things we don't know now!

A "BIGGER PLAN"

Despite all my questions about whatever might be behind the things that I had been experiencing, I had no doubt I was getting the "message" loud and clear, in so many ways, that I was still in a relationship with Shera! Moreover, I felt that it had grown into something new, deeper, and more intimate.

With the regularity and consistency of these events, I found myself awakening to the sense of a Greater Order to life and events at a level I never experienced before.

Now more than ever, I was beginning to understand what I was referring to when I spoke to Shera of a "Bigger Plan."

❖   ❖   ❖

In psychology, there are two classic pictures. The first appears to be of an old hag. However, with a subtle shift of focus it becomes a picture of a young woman. In the second picture, what at first appears to be a vase transforms into two faces looking at each other.

In a similar way, with anything we encounter, a subtle shift of perspective can change what we see and notice, our reactions, our emotions, and the actions we subsequently take.

Consider the change for example, when a joke taken the wrong way is finally explained, or when someone we assumed was a stranger is discovered to be a friend.

CHAPTER 6

A New Balance

A SMILE IS ON MY FACE

A smile is on my face
    tears glistening in my eyes
I hold you in my heart
    and in my thoughts
So many cherished memories
    play before me in my mind
        popping up at random through the days
In these snapshots
    of the times we shared together
        You are beside me still
My sweetheart
    in adventures that we shared
        across the globe
I am so blessed

Yes, you're always with me
    a welcome touch of magic
        in this new life I'm living now
I love you
And in my new life on this new path
    in yet one more adventure
        I'm with you sweetheart,
            once again
And I see and feel your presence
    Flash before me every day
in a holographic record
    that I hold imprinted in my mind
        and in my heart.
So you will be forever with me
    in the memories that I have
of when we explored this world together
    hand in hand
And I give thanks in every day
    for the gift you are to me
        and the delight I feel in knowing
            You are with me still.
I love you.

       ◆   ◆   ◆

I had gone months without writing anything. Upon awakening one morning, I wrote down this poem on impulse. It seemed to just flow out of me. Afterward, as I sat savouring the pleasure of finishing it, I became aware of a persistent tapping.

A small finch, with a blush of pink on its head and neck, was fluttering up repeatedly from the bird feeder outside to tap multiple times on my window. It seemed a little odd. Not having seen this behaviour before, a thought arose in my mind. I heard myself asking out loud, "Shera . . . is that you?"

Immediately, the bird which had been fluttering and tapping persistently for a couple of minutes, stopped abruptly and settled quietly on the feeder.

I was amazed. It had done this at the precise time I asked my question. I thought to myself, although it was half as a request to Shera, "I bet you'll tap one more time to let me know it *is* you."

And in that instant, the beautiful little creature flew once again into the air, and tapped once more on the window—a single gentle tap—and returned to the feeder.

◆　◆　◆

Oh my dear, before you left, in that last powerful week as you lay resting, preparing yourself to go, I had whispered to you, several times, "Shera, send me messages. Let me know how you are doing."

Do you remember? I didn't know what I was really asking for. Reassurance? It was the expression of my hope against hope that our connection was not about to end forever.

Hope was all I had. I had released you to your new life. "Send me an eagle," I said, "or some hearts."

Although you made no sign, I "knew" you had heard me. I had no idea how very well you heard me—or how so much more would come than I could have imagined.

Now, when I would just like to enjoy this new deepening appreciation of you, it feels like the world is pulling at me. There are so many distractions. I fear that I may forfeit the wonder of this connection.

One of those distractions surprises me. I suddenly find myself with a new, somewhat manic curiosity to find out who I am and what drives me . . . even at my age! I'm open to exploring everything in this new search for my core self . . . something on which I can build a new future.

And I have to step up and take whatever risks must be taken to re-engage. With you no longer at my side, it is time now for me to take front and centre. It is time to put my gifts into the world.

I remember wondering after Shera left if we were now forever separated or whether there might be some kind of occasional connection. Of course, I had read accounts of people having contact with "the other side." However, now that I was in this place myself, I wondered if that could happen for me. I was asking myself, "What does connection look like anyway?"

I had no real idea. There are so many ways in which Shera has not left. Endless echoes and reverberations that ripple through my mind and days, bringing hints and sweet touches of her.

I get a sense of some of the reasons why it is a custom in some cultures to gather up and burn everything that belonged to someone who has passed. It is said that the practice frees the departed Soul to continue unencumbered on its way. Paradoxically, there are others who say the fire is a way of sending the things to the departed Soul that it will need to sustain itself and make its way more easily in its new world.

Still, others say it frees the surviving family from the lingering energy and influence of a person's departed Soul that may be carried in the things it had possessed in its time here. All three of these reasons resonate with me. However, I believe ultimately it is the nature of the *relationships* people had with the departed Soul that determine which motivation is most appropriate.

TWO WORLDS

As I write this, I can see that I am caught in two worlds. In one, I find myself in the spontaneous replay of events from a life now gone. In the other, I am dealing with the day to day demands of my current life, which are very present. I am in this world. I move in this world. My body and my feet are on the ground. I see the cars, the streets, the people before me, and sometimes it feels like a dream. But my mind is in another dream, a dream of when Shera, too, was in this place. Beside me. Looking at the things I am looking at.

As I move through my days, it feels like I have this secret life, invisible to those around me. It doesn't seem to be a problem. It's just a little awkward because it is one that those around me cannot reference. I wonder at times whether it is normal.

Shera, too, in my mind at least, is caught in two worlds. She is in another place, another realm, and yet in many ways she is not gone from here. But what does that even mean? I have such a dynamic experience of her passing, and an aching sense of her absence, and yet somehow, she is not gone. She is still here in so many ways.

In my desire to know where Shera is and how she is doing, I want to increase my sensitivity and my intuition to sense her, be with her, and communicate with her more directly, more confidently, and to understand and emulate the Light that guided her.

I vacillate between indifference as I look out on the world continuing on around me, and focussing intensely on the inexplicable things happening in my life: the juxtapositions and coincidences. Other people, dealing with their daily preoccupations, carry on as always, their lives following a well-worn track, unaware that although I stand beside them or sit before them, at times I am not really "here."

MEMORIES

What is so hard, Shera, is having you so very present and so very real in my mind and my life, and yet—I don't even know what words follow here to make sense of what I am saying or feeling. You are so very tantalizingly close!

I am so grateful for these memories. They are like the lingering aftertaste of an exquisite wine. And it is such a blessing to feel your vitality and essence so strongly. What a gift we have been given, you and I, to have lived lives so filled with such treasured moments.

In my mind's eye I see you Shera . . . it is so clear and real. I could be doing anything, reading, cooking, even just resting, when it happens. In a memory that suddenly comes to me, you are real again. I've conjured you up, re-"created" you again. This memory can be so vivid, it is as though I have you standing with me again and we are together—wherever the memory has taken me, perhaps just an afternoon in the living room earlier this year, or maybe in the car beside me on one of our runs to town last year. It could be years ago, trekking with you over the mountains on the Inca Trail in Peru, or riding our elephants in Thailand. In these flashbacks I "see" your face, for just a second or two, usually just a flash, a snapshot, an unexpected visit of you in my mind. Then I'm back again in my new world without you, feeling blessed by a renewed echo of your presence.

It has been quite a ride. So many memories pop up and they can come at any time of the day, regardless of what I am doing. I don't know quite what to make of them. I am surprised. I always thought they would be a source of pain, accentuating my loss of Shera. I imagined them causing distress by reminding me of those things we would never do again.

❖ That is not the case. Instead, I have been delighted at times to find myself suddenly in the middle of a special time we shared, or rediscovering an event I had forgotten. I feel no sadness. The events and adventures we shared were not things we would ever have done again anyway. Instead, I feel so thankful that we had been given the chance to share those experiences at all—and so many of them!

There is a kind of distance in a memory that allows me to see aspects of Shera I did not see before because of whatever distractions and ego-based perspectives I may have had at the time—a time when I was caught up in my own experiencing of those moments. Now I get a new sense of what touched Shera and gave her joy. I can see the special gifts and qualities she had. I can see how those qualities enriched those experiences for me. Basically, these memories give me a chance to see her and appreciate her in ways I had not done before.

For example, one memory took me to the early years of our tours to Peru. Because at that time air travellers were allowed two fifty-pound pieces of luggage each, Shera invited our travellers to fill one suitcase to meet their personal needs for the tour, and fill the second one with used clothing, and toys and games to donate to schools and communities in Peru. At the time, I was occupied with moving bags and piles of clothes. It was always fun in the hotel the first day to sort through the mountain of things everyone had brought. My focus was on managing the space, the people, and the timing, both in the hotel and in the villages where we would be distributing our things in the following days.

Looking back now though, I am reminded it was Shera who had come up with the idea in the first place. I am touched by her vision and how she embraced the opportunity to serve others. Free of the obligations that had captured all my attention at the time, I was now able to appreciate what the project revealed about *Shera*.

I see her in a hotel, in her element, sorting through 400 pounds of clothing piled high behind her. Yet what I see is no longer about the clothes. I see her dedication to service. How deeply she loved the mothers and the children—particularly the children—and how deeply she wanted to help improve lives.

I could see she wanted at some level to correct the imbalance between the excesses we consider normal in Canada, with the poverty and deprivation so common among the people in the mountains of Peru. I could see how she used her masterful sense of cloth, style, and size to pick an item from a jumble of clothes, pants, skirts, or shirts, that would perfectly fit the child or adult she had in mind.

All of these qualities, these values, were things I had not been particularly conscious of as we worked together in the hotels and in the villages of Peru. I saw *what* she was doing, not *why*. That had to wait until I revisited those scenes in my memories. It was then I could see the generous heart and selflessness that motivated her to give birth to the project in the first place.

❖ I believe these unexpected jewels that I have found in the memories that come to me are the reason I have not experienced the pain or distress I had expected to feel. In a way, it as if each of them is reintroducing Shera to me; as if she is revisiting me through these thoughts and memories. Rather than feeling anguish about never being able to do those things again with Shera, with each memory I felt profound *gratitude* that we had been given those moments to share at all.

THINGS

I have had a similar experience with a multitude of "things" I encounter daily that are now in my life. They are a testament to Shera's adventuring spirit that always looked beyond the "familiar" to find new playgrounds to explore. The jiggle machine, infrared sauna, back chairs, crystal bowls, and Tibetan bowls, mementos from Bali Egypt, Thailand, and Peru . . .

There are also those things that I am now safeguarding for Shera's sons: the pottery she made, stained glass, and the antique wooden soy sauce barrels she converted into handmade drums. Her journals and diaries. Personal mementos and heritage items from the ranch in South Dakota she grew up on . . . all unknown to me when she first greeted me on a ferry wharf thirty-four years ago.

I had never given these things much thought. They were just random "bits" Shera kept, bought, or collected at some time. It seems strange to me at some level how they continue on without her. Occasionally, when I notice an item or pick one up, I muse on how many times Shera's hands would have handled them!

They still speak to me of you, Shera.

NOT "THINGS"

❖ Those things are no longer random "things," to me . . . and irrelevant. I may not know their history or how they came to be here, however, since Shera's passing, I find myself paying attention to them in ways I never had before. They offer subtle glimpses into her broader life and history. They reveal insights into her motivation and what gave her comfort and pleasure: a twist of bark or driftwood, the shape and colour of a stone. Feathers. Bones. Fabric.

In the things she gathered to her during her travels through the years, I understand more how she viewed her world and what she valued. How she celebrated life. Some are reminders of the stories she loved to share. Stories that have now become mine to tell. A soapstone scarab beetle I didn't know she had brought from our travels in Egypt. Brightly coloured hand-carved fish from Bali. Knitted finger puppets from Peru. A great many random ceramic mugs, crafts, and weavings.

Yet I was not paying attention to what she was buying and bringing home. In all these items I could now see how motivated Shera was to support the creative work of others wherever she found it. The purchases we made as tourists of some weavings and a pan pipe led to our developing relationships with each of two families of artisans in Peru . . . and to our being becoming godparents to two wonderful children. Those children are now in their thirties!

❖ As with memories, these things of Shera's give me a new lens through which I could view her and the experiences we shared, in a more conscious way. I can better understand the subtle ways she influenced my life. So much of what I now enjoy and appreciate is a direct result of her passion for living life fully, loving Nature, appreciating beauty, and expressing her creativity.

These insights led me to wonder if I had ever really expressed my gratitude to my sweetheart for what she meant to me, and how she had enriched my life. It was uncomfortable to think I might not have. So it was with considerable relief that I came across a card I had given to her that she had carefully kept among her things. It was a handmade card that I had written many years ago. It contained a poem:

> *Shera,*
>
> *Like a petal unfolding from a flower,*
>
> *I am blossoming in the love of you.*
>
> *You are my treasured source of Light and Laughter,*
>
> *a shining Beacon on my Path.*
>
> *When I stand before Beauty*
>
> *You are with me.*

❖ I am so relieved to know that I *had* expressed that to Shera while she was here. I could not improve on the words I wrote then. It so perfectly encapsulates what I feel now, so many years later. I was struck to realize that spite the depth of feeling expressed in this poem, it was written before I could have known how much deeper our love would grow.

❖ *Shera, I wonder what might have been different if I had been more conscious. If I had been more aware earlier all of the many ways that came together to make you the person I loved. Would I have appreciated you more in ways that could have further enriched our relationship. Who knows?*

❖   ❖   ❖

The assumption that death is "the final goodbye" summarizes much of what we are given to believe about the "end" of life. This assumption is also the soil from which the vine of grief grows. Yet it stands at odds with the hundreds—thousands?—of books describing personal experiences of life *after* death, life *before* birth, past life experiences? Or the accounts from people telling of contacts they've had with loved ones who have "died and moved on"?

Imagine if we were to accept these stories into our sense of what is "real," how that would influence the possibility for connection with departed loved ones. Would "relationship" then, in some be more likely after death?

CHAPTER 7

Partners Forever?

Shera, I am still caught in the momentum of your life. Your vision, the magnificent capacity you had to create and transform things, people, spaces. You were "potential" personified, in action, unfolding. You would laugh and say, "When I get an idea . . . ," then as you snapped your right arm out straight, finger pointing away from you, you'd add, "—Swoosh!"

With you there was no space between the inspiration and the execution.

You were always like that. When you moved through your garden things moved with you, random projects moved along. In a thrift store, where others would see shirts and skirts and towels and sheets, you would see people and projects and possibilities unimagined. Where others saw throwaways, you saw an exciting medium. Where others saw driftwood, you saw sculpture.

In addition to the world you lived in and walked through, you lived in a world your mind created from the things you saw and touched. Anything—and anybody—you encountered was a doorway to an unrealized potential. You were like that, right up to your final days.

◆　◆　◆

As the months progressed, the signs I received from Shera appeared less frequently and the nature of the connections changed. In the beginning they were almost daily events. They began immediately after Shera's passing, when I most wanted to know she was still around. They were physical and tangible, often coming as written words as well as "signs" in Nature. Initially, among the other signs I was getting, the Word Bowl particularly, was very busy. Every day or so I could turn to it, looking for "comment" on something that was happening, and it would be there. Every time. Valid. Pertinent.

It became like a touchstone, a dependable reassurance that Shera was not far away. Evidence that she was aware of me and what I was doing. I also had a comforting validation of what I was seeing and also what I was thinking, because many of these events were witnessed by other people.

CHANGES

Over time, as I became more confident that our connection was going to continue, I needed that reassurance less and less. Coincidentally, with that realization, the frequency of the signs and messages dropped off dramatically. The always pertinent word cards from the Word Bowl were less consistently on point. I had moved on.

That was about the time the memories started dropping into my head. At any time of day, I'd find myself spontaneously "visiting" another time and place I had shared with Shera. Again and again. These memories were always positive. Each one renewing my sense of her presence.

❖ Although memories do not come with evidence or witnesses, none were needed. In a sense, each one was just between Shera and me. These "connections" were welcome and valuable. They needed no validation. They gave me new insights into who Shera was and a new appreciation of the relationship we had built together.

Then the random spontaneous memories gradually fell away. I could always choose to visit them, but they seldom leapt to my mind spontaneously. Although I couldn't know it, I had already embarked on the *next* level of connection.

POTENTIAL GONE?

Could Shera really have had so much energy and vitality and momentum, only to have it simply . . . *disappear*? Where had that all that gone? Could it have been ended—erased—just like that? Was such a cruel trick being played? Do we strive our whole lives to develop our gifts and abilities, find our passions and our purpose, expand our knowledge and grow our wisdom, only to have it disappear in a moment? Snuffed out like the flame on a candle, leaving only a wick?

I imagine that many looking at the body of someone deceased see only the "wick," the candle without the light; the body devoid of life and vitality . . . "empty" if you will.

Yet, how can we explain the kind of phenomena I have seen and so many others have experienced? Perhaps it is because our "lenses" are focussed on the "light" of the candle *instead of the wick*? A Soul essence beyond the body? Is it possible that Shera's "flame" continues in another place, her vitality intact?

I know it can be hard to believe, or risky, to attach significance to such coincidences. Many can't entertain the possibility of such things because their beliefs won't allow it. Seeing only the "wick," they keep their conceptual "door" closed to new possibilities. Even if they can accept that these coincidences occurred as I've described them, it can be difficult to allow they have any significance.

The *next* level of synchronicities were less obvious and carried even greater impact.

POTENTIAL UNLEASHED

In my mind, on the night Shera left, her Soul—her life essence—was finally set free to fly on to some other place. However, as events unfolded, it seemed Shera might have decided *not* to "fly on" after all.

In my search to understand the events I have described, I couldn't help wondering if Shera's irrepressible vitality was still able to make changes here. I can come up with no other explanation for how they could be happening. This bizarre idea came to me over time.

It is easy to imagine that once Shera was freed from the limitations of her body, and revitalized, she may well have had other ideas in mind! It is inviting to suppose that after having been relentlessly deprived of the capacity to do anything at all, Shera—as her liberated Soul essence—with a new source of power, influence, and "tools," might have launched herself into a whole new level of involvement and activity! Who's to say?

In any case, it was a year and a half later when I realized that many major changes I had experienced since Shera left *had not been initiated by me*. They were totally unexpected and definitely not planned—and they were transforming my life.

A LIFE CHANGER

Shera never missed an opportunity to encourage someone to pursue their passion. This encouragement could have its impact in an instant or continue over time.

For example, one evening in our home on Galiano, we were having dinner with friends visiting from the States. They were proud parents of a new baby boy. During the conversation, Atah, the father, was sitting with his son on his lap. At one point he shared that he was not happy in his profession as an engineer. "I would like to work with people," he said, and although it was unspoken, it was clear he felt obliged to carry on regardless, in order to support his family.

Although we acknowledged his comment, not much was added and the conversation moved on.

"Shera changed my life that evening," he said later. "When she hugged me goodbye as we left, she whispered into my ear. She told me, 'You know, the greatest gift you could give your son would be to live in your passion.' Ten months later, I was working with people."

Atah had become a life coach.

That kind of encouragement was there for me, as well, from the very beginning of our relationship. Shera could see that words, thoughts, and new ideas were a driving force in me, and she wanted me to share them with the world. To help make that happen, she had become a kind of enthusiastic "sounding board."

I remember her sitting beside me in the car as I drove, listening as I talked about something or other. Suddenly she would grab something—any paper at hand—envelopes, receipts, paper shopping bags—and copy down the gist of what I was saying. She saw me as a writer and a speaker. She imagined me standing in front of people someday. She wasn't going to let my words and ideas be wasted or lost. She was doing everything she could to make sure I would have something to work with later.

For my part, in spite of her efforts, I simply would not see myself as she did. I could not understand, or relate to what she was doing. I did not respond as Atah had done. After a while, Shera stopped taking notes when I was speaking. Yet she never lost her desire to encourage me to live my passion.

Years later, we were standing together one day in the new studio gallery she was building on Salt Spring Island. "You see that?" she asked, drawing my attention to where she had created a platform in a corner of the gallery space. "I see you standing up there sharing your ideas with an ongoing gathering of people who come to hear you speak."

She had never stopped holding that vision of me and my potential.

In spite of her departure, it was as though her intention to support me was continuing on. And the support came in many ways. Events began to unfold one after another. Major changes, all totally consistent with her vision for me as a burgeoning author, started falling into place in a succession of stages—*none of which I initiated.*

HOME SUPPORT

When we had moved into our new home on Salt Spring Island, Shera and I had planned to rent the basement suite. However, it needed a substantial renovation to make that possible. The ceilings needed to be soundproofed. It needed new carpets and a completely new bathroom. With the increasing intensity of care I had been giving Shera in her last three years, a renovation was the last thing I wanted to be thinking about. I knew someday I would have to deal with it. It was an ever-present shadow in my mind.

One day a couple of old friends called me. Shawn and Marilyn wanted to know if I could recommend a bed and breakfast they could stay in while they looked for a place to rent in the longer term. They were planning to move to the island. I said they were welcome to use the unfinished suite downstairs if they wanted to, and explained the situation.

When they arrived, Shera was spending her days in bed. In spite of her being very weak, I was delighted to see how warmly she welcomed them. Unknown to all of us, she was just days away from her decision to leave.

To my great surprise, on their second day, Shawn and Marilyn announced they liked it here. They wanted to rent the space long term. Amazing! In an instant, before I had even thought of looking for them, we had our first renters! *And* I no longer had to think about weeks of renovations!

Their arrival came with an added bonus. Not only did they take up residence, but we also discovered Shawn and Marilyn were energy workers and had practiced esoteric healing work for years. They routinely called on angels and ascended masters for assistance, and for healing and guidance. Although Shera was already on the threshold of her departure, they started work immediately, working in turns from their suite downstairs and at the foot of Shera's bed. Their chanted mantras, and invocations filled the house with a soothing energy that served me as well as Shera.

◆　◆　◆

It was a few days after Shera passed that Ollie arrived. As I navigated my way through my first days and weeks without Shera, these three housemates—Ollie, Shawn, and Marilyn—were like my personal angels. Their patience and open-hearted acceptance gave me the freedom to express whatever I was feeling and thinking as I tried to make sense of what had happened.

When the "coincidences" began happening, I had witnesses rather than sceptics. Day after day, we marvelled together at what was happening. They fully accepted the possibility that these coincidences were indeed "messages" from Shera, and they listened generously and enthusiastically to my stories, my thoughts and new ideas, and my questions. It was as though they had become Shera's proxies, encouraging me to share my voice and insights. I had been given another chance. I had a sounding board again.

This time I was doing something with it! I had finally become the author Shera foresaw, and started recording my conversations *myself.* I didn't want to lose the thoughts and ideas that were coming to me. Wherever she was, I'm sure Shera would have been delighted.

In looking back at how perfectly and seamlessly Marilyn, Shawn, and Ollie had fallen into this role, I was reminded of the way Ollie had been summoned by an eagle. I began to wonder if it was possible that Shawn and Marilyn's arrival could also have been orchestrated by Shera, even before she left her body.

If so, it was just the beginning of her supportive interventions.

A GATHERING

A couple of weeks after Shera's departure, I was feeling totally defeated by the chaos in the gardens she had been developing from the time we purchased our new property on Salt Spring Island, and over the years before we had moved in. She was always a passionate gardener, and for over half a year she became less and less able to tend to them. Now, well into springtime, they had exploded in new growth. Just the thought of dealing with the knee-deep turbulence of weeds oppressed me. Although it *had* to be dealt with, it was the last thing I wanted to do.

I pointed it out to a new friend who was leaving after a short visit. She paused at the door. "Look, I'll come on Saturday and help you, and I'll try to bring a friend or two. Perhaps you could ask friends, as well."

I agreed, although I still knew very few people on the Island. When we had moved into our new home Shera was in a wheelchair. She had just been released from rehabilitation in the hospital following her stroke. We had so much on our plate we hadn't gotten out much into the community. Our energy had been entirely focussed initially on her rehabilitation, and subsequently on dealing with the challenges that came after the cancer returned.

To my amazement, when Saturday came around, *thirteen* people had arrived, keen to get to work! I only knew or had met half of them before! It was a warm sunny day, and people quickly moved into the tasks of cutting the lawn, clearing paths, and weeding the garden beds. I was delighted to notice that in spite of the work needing to be done, it was apparent from the various animated conversations that the "task" had quickly become a social event.

After an hour and a half or so of convivial sharing and working in the various gardens, I served a big lunch. As many of them were complete strangers, I showed them a large picture of Shera. I said wherever she was, she would be delighted because the gardens they were working in had been one of her great passions. Then, after lunch we relaxed into a conversation.

We decided at the outset to ban talk about politics or the pandemic. I suggested each of us share our passions, our insights, and the gifts we were given when we entered into this life. Quite an enlightened conversation followed. It was something Shera and I had always encouraged in the groups of people we worked with.

The conversation seemed to develop a life of its own and went on for an hour and a half. Before people left, they had already decided we would do it again the following Saturday. The gatherings continued every weekend for *five* months!

A couple of weeks later, I was reflecting on how this remarkable situation had unfolded, and I found myself laughing out loud. To my amazement, I realized that within days of Shera's departure, through little fault of my own, not only did I have a new circle of friends, but I was also addressing an ongoing gathering of people on a regular basis—exactly what she had always hoped I would do.

BAIT AND SWITCH

Ultimately, the group came together every Saturday for five months, supporting and learning from each other as they shared passions that ranged from survival camping to numerology and remote viewing. On one Saturday in September, Lynn, who had been with us from the start, announced she felt called to distribute information on the pandemic at the popular Salt Spring Market the following Saturday. As had become our pattern, the whole group dove in to support her. A planning meeting was scheduled the following Tuesday at my home, with Lynn leading.

Our first Saturday was quite successful. The group decided to continue at the Saturday markets, with planning sessions on Tuesdays.

Just as spontaneously as it had begun, the gardening circle came to an end. It had been switched to become an activist group.

As it was still gathering in my home, for the first two meetings, I assisted Lynn. Before the third meeting, Lynn called to say she couldn't make it. She asked me to cover for her. By this time, word had gotten out and over twenty people were attending. Although leading the meeting was a stretch for me, the meeting went well.

So, when Lynn did not attend the next core planning meeting, I was nominated to chair the process of drawing up an agenda for the following general meeting. Although Lynn was at the meeting, she was unfamiliar with the detailed agenda, and I found myself leading the meeting once again.

Three days later, Lynn surprised us all with the announcement that she no longer wanted to be part of the group. She was leaving.

Just like that, it had happened again! Without any particular intention or direct action on my part, I found myself once more leading an ongoing group. However, the laid back, social gardening circle, which had begun in honour of Shera, had suddenly become something quite different; twice as big and growing, it was agenda-driven and challenging. More importantly, in building and shaping the purpose of the group, I was defining and directing it in my own right.

In spite of having had no intention of such a thing at the outset, I discovered an entirely new part of myself, a part which was capable of things I had never attempted before.

Over the next three months, I had thirty people in my living room every Tuesday, organizing events and developing novel initiatives to reach out to people in the community. I worked on creating innovative informational documents for distribution. At one point, I came across an open letter written by a doctor who was taking the Public Health Officer to task for the damage her Covid policies were causing in the community. I converted it into a declaration of protest that could be circulated for signatures. As a courtesy, I sent a copy to the doctor for comment.

To my surprise, in his reply he informed me that he had sent the declaration on to a prominent national health watchdog organization. I had not expected that, and within days I received a call from the president of the organization. As we discussed the declaration, our conversation naturally moved into the current developments. We agreed that government overreach, which in December 2020 was becoming obvious, was only going to get worse. He decided he would convene a national strategy group drawn from activist groups across the country, in order to challenge it.

That is how, within two weeks, I found myself in yet another group. This group was no longer a casual group of people on a small island, it was a morning Zoom call with thirty people participating from around the country. Most of them were leading their own organizations. Every one of them was a credentialed and experienced professional, prominent in their fields. Every one, that is . . . *except me!*

For a long time, my proposed declaration notwithstanding, I believed I had been there largely because I had just happened to be on the call at the time the decision was made to convene the group. I had not recognized that I had been talking to him as the leader of my own, albeit local, "organization!"

Over the next months, I grew accustomed to this new exposure and inspiring company, and felt more at home in this more (to me at least) rarefied air. I moved into two central subgroups, working on their agenda and developing policy and strategies for getting information out globally.

Reflecting on this remarkable succession of circumstances, I realized once again I had been lifted out of my comfort zone. I was working on increasingly bigger platforms at levels I had not known before. I had planned none of this, nor initiated, or even anticipated any of it. As a result I had been led to recognize potential and capabilities in myself I had never allowed myself to own before.

Because all of it had begun after Shera's departure. It was easy to imagine her working somewhere on the other side, pulling strings to make it all happen. Typical.

BECOMING AN AUTHOR

At the Celebration of Life for Shera, I had been profoundly moved by the stories people told of the way she had touched their lives. It was then I began to recognize more fully that her gift to the world had been an ability to encourage and celebrate open-heartedly the creativity and passion in the people she encountered. It seemed "wrong" for this "gift" to end with her departure. I wanted it to continue to benefit others. That was when I decided to write a book that would be part of her legacy.

It was days later that it struck me: barely a week after her passing, writing a book had become my "must do" priority. Shera had always wanted me to honour my potential as a writer, and remarkably, what she had wanted for me from the beginning had finally come together:

I had the inspiration.

I had the motivation.

I had the topic.

And, poignantly, Shera had also removed a major distraction that would have interfered with the project . . . *herself!*

THE JOKE IS ON ME

❖ It took several months before I could see a broad enough context to understand what really happened, and I had to laugh! At the outset, when I decided to get Shera's message out to the public, I had thought that we'd worked the project "together." However, I had forgotten a major piece . . . Shera *always* has her *own* projects independent of mine. In a flash the joke had become obvious: While I on this side worked on "our" projects, Shera on her side was working on *her* project . . . *me!*

Once I had realized this, it became obvious how over the months of coincidences and changes, the way "had been cleared" for me to reach this place I am at now. And I like it! I feel empowered. I'm living more the potential Shera saw in me from the beginning; embracing parts of me that I'd always suppressed or denied.

What she failed to achieve with me while she was alive had come together after all—*starting the moment she left for the other side.* A "coincidence?" Perhaps. I remember that when I realized this, I could almost hear her voice laughing, *"Gotcha!"*

Did I mention? Shera *always* has her own projects! Confirmation came in two telephone calls.

DELAYED DEPARTURE

The first call came from Maria, a new friend calling from Toronto. We had been chatting for a while when she interrupted our session. "Just a moment. Shera is here. She is wanting to say something."

I was intrigued. The conversation had not been about Shera.

Although she was a life coach, Maria has been a natural medium her whole life.

"She is saying that she was supposed to leave three years before she did."

Hearing this, my mind immediately started counting back the years from the day Shera passed. Shera had suffered a catastrophic stroke three years and three weeks before she left! At the time, the doctors told us "She will likely not last three days." They had been quite insistent, "You should let the family know they may have to decide about removing her from life support."

I had never told Maria anything about Shera having a stroke! I turned my attention back to what she was saying.

"She says she decided to stay," Maria continued, "because she wanted to make sure you would be okay."

Shera and I had barely sold our home of over thirty years at the time of the stroke. If Shera had indeed left at that time, I would quite literally have been left "home"less and devastated, taking up residence in a house I had zero connection with, the empty echoes of a vision and plans that had just evaporated, and mountains of *things* piled around me.

Remarkably, unknown to Maria, at some point shortly before her passing I had actually thanked Shera for staying with me for those three years. I told her they had been a huge gift to me. For the first half of those years, Shera made huge strides in recovering from her stroke. We had started implementing our vision for the place, making it ours. We built a greenhouse, extended the gardens, started remodelling the house. We got the gallery up and running.

Over that time, I became fully bonded with this new place. It had indeed become my *home*. However, until Maria had given me Shera's message, I had no idea that had actually been Shera's intention.

The call certainly corroborated my sense that Shera had indeed been with me, clearing my way so to speak for quite a while—from three years before her passing! It was not hard to believe that her hand had been behind the many changes in my life since.

"A DEAR UNFINISHED TASK"

It was seven o'clock in the morning on the second anniversary of Shera's passing. To mark the significance of the day, I was sitting quietly in honour of Shera, holding a space for her in my heart and thoughts. Some candles were burning beside me. I was feeling gratitude for her life and all I had experienced since she left. I could feel she was close by.

That was when there was a "ding" from my cellphone. An interruption.

Of all the days in a year, and hours in the day, it was at this early hour on this special day, that a friend happened to be musing about the thousand books in her library. She got an impulse to pick one book out—the smallest book—and look at it. A tiny book of poems. When she opened it, one poem caught her eye.

She said later, "I didn't know what day it was, but I woke up with the idea of looking through my library. When I noticed this book and opened it, I just knew it was the right thing for you to be reading. Quite honestly, I feel like Shera orchestrated that through me."

I clicked on the image of the poem on the phone before me:

> *If I should die and leave you here a while,*
>
> *be not like others—sore undone,*
>
> *Who keep long vigils by the silent dust and weep.*
>
> *For my sake turn again to life and smile,*
>
> *Nerving thy heart and trembling hands*
>
> *To do something to comfort weaker hearts than thine*
>
> *Complete those dear unfinished tasks of mine*
>
> *And I perchance may therein comfort you.*

Every sentiment expressed fit me perfectly—*line by line!* I was stunned and profoundly moved! I have always considered my separation from Shera was only for "a while."

I had not been "sore undone" by the grief one might have expected me to have.

I am indeed "nerving my heart and . . . hands to comfort" others finding their way after the loss of a loved one . . . by writing this book.

The next line, "Complete those dear unfinished tasks of mine," seemed oddly out of place in a poem of consolation. Yet it was a perfectly fitting reference to the two "dear unfinished tasks" of Shera's that had naturally fallen to me after her passing. Her newly opened studio/gallery, and of course the vegetable gardens she so loved, had both fallen to me to manage. Needless to say, any time I spent on either of these "tasks" would give rise to thoughts of Shera that "comforted" me.

For months, that was how I shared the story. Then, six months later, I received a call from Nick.

Nick was a young volunteer who had worked with us for a few months the year before Shera passed. Shera discovered he had a passion for writing, and in no time she made it a priority to encourage him to keep going with his writing and to finish the book he said he had started. I was reminded of those times when Shera had played the same role with me, so earnestly encouraging me to write. Nick, however, was totally receptive, and by the time he left us, he was fully intent on writing the book she knew was in him to write.

Nick was phoning to ask if he could stop by for a visit. I was pleased to hear from him. We had only connected once or twice in the four years since he had been here. He wanted me to be one of the first people with whom to celebrate the imminent publication of his newly-completed book.

While he was here, I told the story and read the poem I had received. This young author, whose story as Shera's protégé mirrored mine, listened intently, and when I was finished he paused a moment, looking straight into my eyes before commenting. Then, he raised his eyebrows and a bemused smile spread across his face.

"You know what Shera is talking about, don't you?"

I was confused. "What do you mean?"

He laughed, "*You* are one of her 'dear unfinished tasks!'"

I was speechless. Clearly, when I had first read that poem on that morning months earlier, I had missed a key piece of the "message" Shera intended for me. So she sent it again! This time it was delivered to me in person, concisely, *by the perfect messenger:* another author she had motivated to write the book that was in them to write—*a virtual clone of myself.*

◆　　◆　　◆

The Third Lens—
How Can This Be?

The experiences I've had, and this ongoing connection with Shera, were not things I had expected. I had not thought much before about contacts after death, and certainly had no idea how common they might be. Was it all happening totally by chance? Was it something about me? Something I did?

In my quest to understand what happened during and after Shera's departure, I became aware of several things that would likely have contributed to make the connection that developed more possible.

Through this third lens you can see the things I was doing after Shera passed which sustained the sense of her continuing presence, and which, I believe, made me more sensitive to the contact events when they happened.

It is said that we are only given in life the things we are able to handle. Does that mean we are already being prepared and equipped for whatever may come? . . . gifts as well as challenges?

As a rule, the demands of our days keep our attention focussed on what we need to deal with in the moment.

It is in the challenge of a loved one's passing that we are given a rare opportunity to look beyond the world we see before us every day, and gaze into the Mystery that has captivated the imagination of people since the beginning of time.

And in this time when our world has changed, in this reordering of our life, we can reconsider what a loving relationship can become.

CHAPTER 8

Staying In Touch

"Everything you love will probably be lost,
but in the end, love will return in another way."
Franz Kafka

❖   ❖   ❖

After the loss of someone dearly loved, it is no wonder someone might feel "alone" in ways others may not understand. After all, any loving relationship is a daily dance through many emotions, expectations, and exchanges, which also become part of the loss.

THE DANCE CONTINUES

When Shera left, I had no idea what lay ahead. I did not immediately comprehend the implications of her departure. Certainly, I knew I was in a new world, and although a part of me hoped there may be some sort of sign from her, I certainly had no expectation it would happen.

So, when the surprising coincidences I have described started happening, I had no sure explanation for them. Certainly, the easiest explanation for all of it was to imagine Shera's "hands" were at work, although I leave you to make your own determination on that. Be that as it may, I sensed her *presence* in all that unfolded.

I immediately began to see, with fresh eyes, what she brought together in her life, and the things she had done. Beyond the "three-dimensional" personality and ego I knew so well, I'd been getting a clearer sense of her Soul's essence as never before. By "Soul" I mean the vital, enlivening energy that was the source of her passions, her vision, and her purpose, and how she expressed them through the body she had just left. Indeed, I am actually loving her now in ways that would have been virtually impossible if she were still alive and beside me.

> *Her Soul is the enlivening energy that was the source of her passions, her purpose, and how she expressed them.*

With so many "signs" and "messages" since her passing hinting at her continuing presence, I have come to believe, as I have shared already, that I have not "lost" Shera. I am dancing on with her in a new meaningful "*relationship.*"

The question is, "How did that happen?"

In my quest for an answer, I have identified several things which I believe contributed to making it possible. Things I believe and things I was doing. By sharing them here, I hope they may help others feeling the loss of a loved one find a way to having a similar experience.

TUNING IN: EMPATHY

I had never realized how, in Shera's last months, my days had become defined by the habits and routines we shared. As she became increasingly less able to say what was going on for her, I developed the ability to anticipate what she was thinking. Rather than focussing only on the words she was trying to say, I tuned into what she was wanting to share. At times it was like managing both sides of a conversation.

This also meant that while she was still here with me in the body, I was already becoming more sensitive to subtle, non-verbal, and energetic signs she was giving me. I believe this sensitivity may have primed me to recognize some of the "messages" that were to come. I believe that is why, after she passed, as I was framing my thoughts and my writing, I continued to have Shera in mind.

In this context, it is worth mentioning how the house itself, filled with so much of what "spoke" of her—her art, her passions, her history her favourite collectibles—seemed inherently to hold or "carry" messages, if not from her, certainly about her. At times I felt much of what she had collected became almost a proxy for her being here. I would feel her in her things and in the memories they evoked.

Writing implied a listener I was writing to.

As a result, I did several things I would quite naturally have done if she were still with me.

1. CONTINUING THE CONVERSATION

For weeks and months after Shera's departure, I found myself spontaneously writing poems and letters to her. I have shared many of these writings as introductions to earlier chapters in this book. Notwithstanding her departure, I was addressing them to a woman I loved, and whom I still love and care about. Using her name—writing *to* her—created an illusion that she was somewhere listening to me. Getting my message. Hearing my questions. It gave me a comforting sense of continuity.

Most importantly, I was continuing the conversation. I realize now how holding up *my* side of the conversation, so to speak, predisposed me to be receptive to any response, if there should be any, that may come from her side.

Directed Journalling

After Shera left, I had so many thoughts, so many questions. There were so many things going on emotionally, and with all the thoughts crowding my mind, I didn't want to lose them. I began journaling in earnest for the first time in my life. I was writing every day to help myself hold things in perspective. It helped me understand what I was feeling. I could examine what I believed and become more aware of what I was expecting. So much was completely new, I didn't want to miss something important. These writings became the starting point for the reflections and insights I share in this book.

> *In sharing whatever was going on for me*
> *I would often gain clarity.*

I quickly discovered they also gave me a considerable degree of comfort. Writing as I did implied a listener, someone I was writing *to*. So, quite naturally my journalling became a kind of surrogate conversation with Shera, a conversation I might have held with her in person about what was going on. It was easy to feel she might be listening somewhere, interested in my thoughts, challenges, and insights.

Non-Dominant Handwriting

I found this exercise to be valuable at times when I was looking for more substantial feedback. It is a Gestalt therapy technique Shera used with clients in her healing practice. It goes beyond a simple "Yes" or "No" response and offers a way of accessing the subliminal knowing of one's native wisdom. It could be described as a kind of internal channelling.

I would begin by writing whatever question I had on a page of paper, using my right hand (my dominant writing hand). Then transferring the pen to my non-dominant left hand, I would write whatever reply, words, or thoughts were triggered by the question. When the response was complete, I would move the pen back to my dominant hand again and write another question.

Often, the insights I would get were quite remarkable. The exercise helped sustain the possibility in my mind of a meaningful contact with Shera.

Letter Writing

At times, as events and questions built up in the days following Shera's departure, I discovered that just spontaneously writing a letter to her was hugely satisfying as a way to express doubt or confusion, and to release the pressure of the moment. In sharing whatever it was that going on for me, as I had done so many times over the years we lived together, I would often gain the clarity I was looking for about whatever the issue might have been. This also helped sustain the sense of Shera's energy and continuing presence.

Pendulum

Most people are aware of this phenomenon, as it is used in the hands of people who work with a forked stick to dowse for water. Pendulums are a way to amplify a subliminal "knowing." Using a stone or crystal on a string, both Shera and I have successfully dowsed for the best places to drill wells, and found an excellent supply of water on every occasion.

Pendulums are a way of amplifying a subliminal "knowing."

I first heard of pendulums years agom when I saw people using them for guidance and getting answers to questions. At its most simple form, a question is directed to the object suspended on the string. In "response," the object spontaneously begins to spin in a circular motion or swing back and forth in ways that indicate "Yes" or "No." It was remarkable how consistently the answer would prove to be correct.

After Shera left, I thought of using a pendulum to "connect" with her and find answers to some of the unanswerable questions that came up, and to get a sense of how she was and what was happening with her. It was also a way to satisfy myself that something I had thought might be a message from Shera was indeed a message from her. Using the pendulum had the effect of giving her a voice in the "conversation," so to speak.

Whether the "answers" were credible communications or not, who is to say? However, I believe this exercise, along with the other things I mentioned above, all helped set a context in which I was maintaining an emotional and energetic "contact" of sorts with Shera. I have no doubt they also prepared me to recognize and receive the contacts that were to come.

Holding A Space

In the immediacy of Shera's absence, I found it was the most natural thing to take some of the things that had defined Shera's passion and daily routine, special items and photos she treasured, tokens of her different gifts and essences, and assemble them on her dresser. This effectively created a "memory corner" that evoked a sense of Shera and represented many of the essences and relationships she valued.

> *Simply sitting quietly by a lit candle would often give me the feeling she was nearby.*

On special occasions, simply sitting quietly by a lit candle placed by these things of hers would often give me the feeling she was nearby.

2. ACKNOWLEDGING A BIGGER PICTURE

It is worth noting that none of these things I have discussed here which helped make it possible for me to experience the ongoing presence of Shera, is particularly remarkable or unique. That is essentially why I believe some kind of "connection" with a loved one that has moved on is within the reach of anyone. What these actions have in common is a willingness on my part to reach out *as though communication with Shera were still possible.* I believe this created a subliminal readiness to recognize and receive responses from her when they came.

In addition, there were other things I suspect played a greater role, beyond anything I was saying or doing.

Energy Shift

During each of our healing sessions over the many months of working with Shera, at some point I had called on God and angels for help in Shera's healing. Whether I was aware of it or not at the time, in this simple act I had begun shifting energetically and psychically to align with whatever invisible "Powers" or forces that may be.

I came to understand, and believe, that each of us is an energy force occupying a physical body. This made it easier for me to accept that when Shera left her body, her life energy would continue in a spirit body. It felt quite natural to continue to direct my thoughts and words to her.

> *I found myself surrendering to something beyond my capacity to understand.*

A Higher Vibration

Looking back, I am amazed at how constant my thoughts and beliefs became over the time I was coping with Shera's departure. When all we had done for her recovery failed, I could have become caught in any of several emotions: anger, sadness, grief, frustration. Yet I found myself surrendering instead to something I knew was beyond my capacity to understand, something I called a "Bigger Plan," a Higher Order in which there are no mistakes. When Shera passed, this belief that there is a bigger plan which is part of a divine order led me quite naturally to the assumption that in moving into spirit, she was also moving to a higher frequency/vibration.

I think that is why when Shera passed, I found myself feeling humility . . . and acceptance. I felt gratitude for the blessing she had been to me during our lives together.

Because humility, acceptance, and gratitude are higher vibrational emotions, they made me more attuned energetically to the frequencies where Shera was in spirit. If instead I had let myself be caught in feelings of despair, sadness, anger, blame, or guilt, all of which are certainly understandable options, they would have lowered my frequency and taken me out of resonance with Shera. I believe this contributed energetically to the sensitivity I had to what I came to recognize as contacts and messages from Shera.

3. HAVING CONFIDENCE IN MY EXPERIENCE

I had no way of proving absolutely the first event I took to be a "sign" from Shera was indeed a message from Shera. I also had no idea if it would be the only one I would get. I certainly didn't know they would continue over a longer period of time. However, I *did* know without question that what happened *had* happened. What I felt and experienced had indeed happened.

Many people are able to feel the presence of their loved one.

I believe over time, holding to this simple premise meant that although others—even I—may question the meaning or significance of an event, I could describe whatever it was unapologetically, because it did happen. The ability to have, hold, and declare what I experienced, even though I feared others might doubt or dismiss it, helped me gain the confidence that enhanced my ability to recognize signs and communications when they happened. I discuss this more later in Chapter 11.

As my confidence grew, it made it possible to write this book as I have.

Over time, as contacts continued, I learned to recognize what a connection could "look" like. With Shera, in the beginning it was often word cards. (Chapter 5: Word Play) Other times it was an eagle. (Chapter 5: Eagles) It could also be a token object—a bird, a feeling, a spontaneous thought or memory, a song, a smell—and I would *know* she was present, even though I could neither see nor hear her. (Chapter 10: Plan Ahead) More importantly, I learned what a communication from a loved one *feels* like.

Sensing Presence

Many people, even those who may not yet recognize "communications" as such, are able to feel the "presence" of their loved one and become convinced their loved ones are nearby, because their extrasensory perception is picking up on them.

> *People who may not see signs, often sense a "presence."*

My most remarkable instance of sensing Shera's presence came with immediate confirmation. I had walked halfway to the top of a local mountain, intending to spend three days and nights in isolation on a kind of vision quest. I stopped there at a lookout point and sat down on some moss at the edge of a cliff. On this sunny autumn day, the expansive view of the ocean and islands below was spectacularly crisp and clear.

In this beautiful moment, buffeted gently by the wind, I suddenly found myself thinking of Shera. I could feel her presence so strongly I could almost see her above me. Playing with the sensation, I physically lifted my butt off the moss where I was sitting and shifted a few inches to the left. In my mind's eye I was making room for Shera to sit down beside me, and I patted the moss with my hand as an invitation to her to join me. I remember smiling to myself that I would do such a thing. I'd never done anything remotely like it before or since.

The confirmation was immediate. As I turned my attention forward again, a strange small grey *blur* caught my eye. It was in the middle of the golden moss by my feet. Intrigued, I reached out to extract it from the moss and cradled it in my hands. Once there, it came into focus; no longer reduced to a blur by the wind blowing over it. It was a small feather that had been snagged in the moss. A fluffy down feather . . . of an *eagle!*

Most of the time only you will be able to validate the experience.

It is important to learn to trust what you are experiencing is real *because* you are experiencing it. We are talking about communication with a "world" that works by rules different from the ones we are used to. Much will be new, and much of it virtually indescribable, because it is a world of energy; a world without form that does not translate easily into terms understandable in a physical reality.

> ### *Most of the time only you will be able to validate the experience.*

Most of the time, you are the one and only reference point and "authority" in what is essentially a personal communication between two people—you and your loved one. *Only you* will know and be able to validate the experience.

4. CELEBRATING WITH OTHERS

With Friends

With Shera's passing, I found myself living in an altered reality only I could see. In my case, if someone had asked me at the time, I would have expected to be forlorn and saddened by grief at losing her. Certainly, this was borne out by the intense pain and anguish I felt upon bringing her ashes into the house from the crematorium.

Yet the extraordinary events I describe in Chapter 5: Letter From Heaven, and in the days following, so convinced me of Shera's continuing presence, my grief at "losing" her largely vanished. The succession of "messages" from Shera even had the effect of making me upbeat and positive. As this new reality of an ongoing connection became an undeniable part of my life, I became more and more excited about the implications of it.

Yet, I felt awkward or uncomfortable with strangers at the beginning, when I tried to talk about my experiences. I was concerned that what was so real and vivid to me may not mean much to anyone else. My experiences might be seen as bizarre by others, and dismissed outright.

However, my first "audience" had been Ollie, Shawn, and Marilyn, the three people in my household who were keenly interested in the events I was experiencing. They had even witnessed some of them. I could safely and freely share my thoughts and feelings.

They were enthusiastically attentive to everything I shared about the communications I was receiving, and the insights that came to me as a result of them. There is no doubt that this book was made possible by those months of sharing, and the "spirited" conversations that followed. (Chapter 6: Home Support)

Most people, even complete strangers
were curious and wanted to know more.

Creating an "inner circle" of friends as I did, would be such a blessing to anyone in my situation—in many ways. For example, in my case:

- I quickly developed confidence in what I was seeing, and in my interpretation of events.
- It helped me to normalize and internalize the exceptional events I was experiencing.
- It made it easier to recognize subsequent contacts when they came.
- It enabled me to uncover aspects and insights of an event which I might otherwise have missed.

With Strangers

I am sure the open acceptance I received from my housemates made it much easier for me to share with anyone. I began to share my stories, with visitors to Shera's gallery.

That was how I discovered most people, even complete strangers, actually were open and willing to listen. They were curious and wanted to know more. I was surprised and enormously delighted at the number of people who would respond to my stories with accounts of their own! In fact I don't recall anyone being dismissive or having a negative reaction to what I was saying.

A WORD ABOUT GRIEF

What happened in my case? I certainly experienced an unbearable paroxysm of grief when I returned home from the crematorium with her body's ashes in my arms. (Chapter 5: A Letter From Heaven) Yet from that time on, any sadness I would feel was generally mild and short-lived. Why? Because when Shera's joyful image appeared in my hands with such perfect timing, I could only believe it was a direct message from her. In that instant the extraordinary distress and grief that had engulfed me, completely evaporated. From that moment on, I *knew* Shera had not gone away, and was still nearby.

Grief is Love with nowhere to go.

Since then, instead of the regret and grief I had expected to feel, my thoughts and emotions were most often of gratitude and love. The degree of loss I had felt before that moment in my living room, holding the ashes, was never able to return.

In reflecting on what had happened, I realized that grief had hit me the hardest in the instant I became finally convinced I would *never again be able to share my love with her and tell her I loved her.* It meant all the love I held for her had nowhere to go.

However, after that transformative moment in my living room, I carried the subliminal assumption that she was not far away. I had also quite unwittingly found a way to continue "actively" loving her in everything I wrote, and what I shared with friends. It all helped to nurture a sense of her *continuing* presence.

Without knowing it at the time, as I subsequently began to *expect* "messages," I was further reinforcing the sense that Shera had not left; that she was still with me, listening and watching. In my journalling, my writing, and the work with the pendulum, I was unconsciously reaching out to her . . . including her.

I had no idea how profoundly this would shape my perceptions, thoughts, and emotions. My sense of "losing" my life partner effectively disappeared. I loved her more than ever, and the grief I had felt quickly became little more than occasional pangs of sadness or poignancy.

It is well understood in science that the brain is a blind servant. Joe Dispenza, Bruce Lipton, and Gregg Braden for example, all teach that the brain will "believe" whatever it is told. Simply by changing what we think and believe, we can change the way we experience the world. That is, in part, what happened for me. The interactive tone of my writing after Shera left, convinced my brain she was not far away. Effectively, by engaging in this ongoing "conversation" with her, I was *causing* her to be present—in my mind at least.

Love is held hostage by grief.

I believe this was perhaps the single most important aspect of what I was doing that enabled me to recognize and receive the messages which I have described in this book. It is why I believe it is within the reach of others in a similar situation to build an ongoing sense of connection with someone who has passed on. This alone will shift their frame of mind—*and their grief*—as it did mine, and open them to receive signs and signals of connection that may be coming their way.

For those feeling the loss of a beloved spouse, friend, child, or parent, the hardest challenge is Grief itself. It holds love hostage.

It is a cruel paradox. The word "grief" alone creates contraction both physically and emotionally. Intuitively, I knew I had to free myself from this tight feeling of loss. It blocks the expression of love. Love is expansive. It knows no barrier of time or place. It is a "high frequency" emotion which lifts energy and raises the vibration. That is why people in love with each other are often a gift to everyone around them, brightening the space and softening the energy. Feelings of love resonate with Spirit.

Recording my thoughts was a way of expressing my love.

Because writing is such a natural way for me to express myself, recording my thoughts easily became a way of expressing my love. As I moved more into expressing love, I was lifting my vibration by loving more and grieving less. This aligned me more with the higher vibration of Shera and where she is now. Most people do this intuitively, and it can be done in other ways. They may walk in a forest, or along a river or by the ocean, for example, with a departed loved one in mind. They may express their gratitude and love *out loud*. They take time to reflect or meditate. All of this is high frequency activity. It raises the energetic vibration and enables better resonance with someone who is in spirit.

In my case, even now, at times when I am doing or observing something Shera and I would have enjoyed together, I often recite out loud what I wrote to her in a poem, "When I stand before beauty you are with me"—*and she is!*

◆　◆　◆

THE TAKEAWAYS

❖ Continuing to express love to a departed loved one can help reduce the intensity of grief.

❖ Love is expansive. It lifts the vibration.

❖ Love opens an energy "channel" which enables connection with loved ones in spirit on the other side.

❖ Continuing the "conversation" with a departed Soul, in whatever form that takes, creates a sense of their ongoing presence.

The Fourth Lens— Getting The Message

In our modern world, thousands of things vie for our attention all the time. For example, it is estimated the average person in a city is exposed to thousands of advertisements and messages in a day—in addition to all the other things that swirl around them! How then is it possible, in such an ocean of competing stimuli, to recognize and receive the subtle signs and messages a loved one may be sending?

Through this lens, I examine the elements of this new mode of communication, and what makes it stand out from the turbulent backdrop of the physical world.

You will also see ways to better notice the signs and recognize them as messages, despite the extraordinary range of forms or shapes in which they might appear.

Any channel of communication has three essential elements: the Sender, the Receiver, and the Channel through which the communication is sent. While we may think the Sender, in this case the departed loved one, is the most important piece, the other two elements are no less important.

What would you do, for example, if someone you wanted to hear from was trying to communicate with you, but you were unable to hear them, no matter how loudly they shouted? This may well describe the challenge faced by Souls on the other side who are wanting to reach out to loved ones they left behind. They may be waiting for us to get a hearing aid.

For such communication to succeed, we have to improve our ability to hear.

CHAPTER 9

Communication

She is not lost your dearest love
Nor has she travelled far,
Just stepped inside Home's loveliest room
And left the door ajar.

Anon

◆　　◆　　◆

This has been such an amazing time. I've learned so much.

At the beginning of this adventure, before Shera left, and before this journey became a quest, I had asked Shera to send me a sign now and then, to "keep in touch" so to speak, and to let me know how she was. I have no idea how much I really believed at that time such a thing might actually happen.

It's natural, of course, to believe this desire to keep some kind of contact with Shera, however tenuous, was based in love. Upon reflection, it was more likely an unconscious manoeuvre to postpone having to accept the finality of her departure. The love I felt as I spoke those words was inextricably bound with the fear of the pain and grief that would inevitably follow if I ever had to admit Shera was irrevocably "dead and gone." In some convoluted logic, as long as I could continue hoping for some kind of contact from her, I could continue to believe she had not finally "gone." As long as I might see an eagle, Shera's totem animal, or come across hearts on a poster somewhere, I could avoid drawing that black line across my life that would consign her forever to the past.

I preferred to believe she had just "flown on" to her new adventure. Out of sight perhaps, but hopefully not out of "touch."

***We assume connection depends on the
one who has departed.***

IT TAKES TWO TO TANGO

Understandably, those who believe contact with a departed loved one may be possible, can become disappointed if it does not happen for them. The *absence* of signs or messages may leave them feeling left behind or abandoned. It can give rise to uncomfortable questions and thoughts that could even deepen their grief:

"Why haven't I received any signs?"

"Why is there no contact?"

"Maybe they don't want to make contact."

"Perhaps our love was not all I thought it was, or they had other things to do and simply moved on."

I suspect that is why many people give up hoping for the contact they would dearly like to have. It's easy to believe it would be less painful, to just accept the departed loved one is simply "dead and gone."

However, the reason there appears not to have been contact may be the assumption that connection depends on the one who has departed.

After all, if there's going to be a "message" *they'd* have to send it first, right?

This is only partly correct. As I was implying in the previous chapter, having connection depends—perhaps even more—*on the one left behind.* "But," you ask, "How can that be? What could I do to get *them* to send signs and messages?"

Think about it though. If you are hoping to get a phone call from a friend, for example, it doesn't matter how often they dial—*if you don't pick up the phone, you won't receive the call.* Even if messages *are* being sent, you have to be open and prepared to "receive" the contact.

You need to believe it is possible to become a Receiver.

In most cases, it is the long-standing social conditioning since we were children that leads many of us to doubt or outright disbelieve connection after death is possible. In any case, it would be too disheartening to go on and on believing and hoping for signs that may never come. Anyone in such a state of mind would be unlikely to receive a message even if one came. They wouldn't be able to hear their "phone" ringing.

That is what happened to Matt in the following story.

OPEN TO RECEIVE

Shortly after Shera left, the first visitor to visit Shera's gallery shared a captivating story:

I have two nice neighbours, Matt and Christa, a really nice couple who were always building things and fixing things. We'd have these very deep conversations in a very odd way, just chatting over the fence . . . really nice conversations . . . really connected.

I particularly felt connected to Christa, the wife. Then, at one point she said, "I want you to know I have terminal cancer."

That was really horrible news. I think she was in her mid-forties. Not long after that, she died.

After that, I could see Matt going into his garden, now by himself. He had aged twenty years. He was hunched. He was just destroyed. He was just so enveloped in his grief there was not a lot of room to talk—he was just encapsulated in this grief.

Then maybe a month or so later—I started having dreams of Christa, sleeping dreams, and she's like, "Sharon. Sharon, I'm trying to get Matt's attention. Can you please tell him I'm trying to get his attention? I keep doing things in front of him, but he keeps turning away."

And she was showing me these images and I'd say to myself, "I can't do that . . . that's just like—What!? This is just a dream!"

But Christa would keep coming back and say, "Please tell him! Can you give Matt this message that I'm trying to contact him, and I want to speak with him?"

So, I took Christa's message seriously, although I felt a little uncomfortable because I had no idea what his belief system was. One day, I mustered up my courage and I was like, "Hi Matt."

And he's like, in very subdued voice, "Oh . . . hi Sharon."

And I said, "So I'm not sure how you're going to take this . . . I feel a little uncomfortable. I just wanted to let you know that I've had this dream—a number of dreams—about Christa. She's trying very hard to contact you and give you messages and show you that she's around you. But she says that you're so distracted and sad she's unable to get to you directly so she's asked me to step in for her."

Long weighted pause, like—I didn't know what was going to happen. There are silences you fill with your own meaning if you don't get a response. And this seemed like a very long silence. I was like, "Oh my God, here it goes."

And then he said, "Oh . . . well . . . thank you. Thank you for letting me know."

It wasn't long after that he decided to go see a hypnotherapist, and she was able to take him back into a very relaxed state where he was able to very easily connect with Christa! He was having absolutely direct conversations, it wasn't like little bits and pieces. He became so enraptured with this idea, and so certain that she was present, at one point he said, "It's like you're not even dead!"

She came back as, you know, her own snappy, humorous, self. She said, "Well that's funny, because if I'm not dead, why are you the one who always has to take the dog out for walks now?"

She assured him that, you know, she was no longer in pain and that she was okay, and she was concerned for him, and he had to go on and was going to be okay. So, he was able to stop going to the hypnotherapist and just connect in his own way, and just converse with her.

Everything about him changed after that, like, his body, his stance, and everything, because he knew that she was still there to talk to when he needed her. He could stay in the relationship and stay connected to the here and now, as well.

It allowed him to move on. He eventually remarried and I'm sure he's still in touch with Christa.

To avoid the pain of having lost the woman he loved, he shut down his own love.

LOVE UPSIDE DOWN

There is so much to be gleaned from this remarkable story. After Christa died, it was as though Matt shut down a vital piece of his life and Soul. Although totally understandable, it was a misguided expression of the depth of his love. The love he had lived and expressed to Christa every day for years and years. That love did not end because Christa was "gone." It just had nowhere to go. He couldn't express it. Instead of celebrating the love he had for his beloved Christa, he felt the pain from being unable to express that love. It seemed pointless. "It's done." With that thought, Matt had fallen into profound grief and abandonment.

He had made a different, albeit unconscious, *choice*. He chose to block his feeling completely. In attempting to avoid the pain of losing the woman he loved, he shut down his own love. In such a state there was zero likelihood he would be able to recognize a sign from Christa. It a tragic cycle of grief. He had simply created more pain.

He had effectively dismissed any chance he might have had to receive the one thing he wanted most: connection with Christa. As Sharon described it, Matt lost his ability to relate to life itself. He had shut down his heart. His love. His life. Figuratively, he had set aside the "phone" he needed to receive her calls.

Love does not end with death, either for the survivor or the departed Soul.

Without the message relayed to him by Sharon, he might never have discovered Christa had not gone away. He would never have known she still loved him deeply, *or that he could continue to love her.*

Unlike Matt, I had never said, "That's it. It's finished. Shera's gone."

When I asked her for "a sign, an eagle or hearts," I was unwittingly putting myself into receiving mode. In a sense, I was turning on my "phone." I was able to receive the signs and messages which started coming, and all the events which have unfolded since Shera passed. That has led me to the wonderful sense of our ongoing connection . . . and has enabled our *relationship* to continue.

LOVE GOES BOTH WAYS

I believe those who have gone ahead continue to care for us. They still love us. They want us to be happy and to thrive. Sharon's story highlights four of the most important things I have discovered in this quest:

- Love does *not* end with death, for the survivor nor the departed Soul.
- Love knows no boundaries of time nor distance.
- Love is the language of the Soul.
- Love goes *both* ways.

While Matt was in his grief and feeling his loss, his love became a source of deep pain. However, he was not the only one hurting. Christa clearly felt his pain as well. She desperately wanted to reach him and let him know she was okay. She wanted to help him stop hurting so much. She wanted to reassure him she was watching him, that she was nearby and loved him still. *She wanted to let him know he could still love her!*

Love has no limit in time or space.

As much as we may want to feel the love of someone who has passed, they too will feel and be nurtured by the love we direct to them, wherever they are. As I indicated in the last chapter, I did not stop expressing the love I had for Shera. And as a result, despite her departure, I continued to feel I was in "relationship" with her.

The key, I believe, is to stay open to feeling—and expressing—love for the one who has left, in spite of the pain of losing their *physical* presence. For me, shutting my love down for Shera would have been far more painful than continuing to love her as I have. I would have been in a similar situation to what happened to Matt.

Christa's love was able to find the way to help Matt turn on his "phone," so to speak, so he could receive again—and when he did, *he* came back to life!

THEY CARE — AND YOU CAN, TOO

Those who have gone ahead want loved ones they have left behind to thrive. They can even play a support role in different ways and to different degrees, as I described in all that Shera has done for me. They can also play a protective role.

Our goddaughter, Magaly in Peru, related to me an uncomfortable situation she found herself in a few weeks after her father passed on. She was alone one evening, when a stranger approached her, acting in a way that made her feel threatened. Unsure what she could do, she closed her eyes and called on help from her father. In the next moment, another person appeared. Although he too was a stranger, he walked right up to Magaly and engaged in conversation with her. With his arrival the threat from the first person ended. Magaly said she believed the friendly stranger had been sent by her father.

Their love continues even after they have departed.

Love has no limit in time or space. It passes across the "veil." There are countless stories told, and books written, which demonstrate spirits are watching from the other side. It's worthy to note, for example, it is the *spirit* who comes forward to make themselves known to a medium. Those on the other side are aware, watching, and looking for opportunities to make contact. They want to establish a connection with their loved one who has gone to work with the medium. Their love continues even after they have departed.

It may be hard to believe such things are possible, yet beliefs can change—a good example of this is Matt in Sharon's story. I discuss this more in Chapter 13. After a few visits with the hypnotherapist, Matt no longer felt the need for an intermediary. He continued in connection with Christa, in "conversations" with her every day. Confident of his connection, he was able to share his love again.

One session with a medium can be enough to make someone a "believer," as happened with Mark. Or, as happened with me, it might be a single event. Many people I have spoken to have readily shared their story of a treasured event which proved to them that the one they "lost" was still with them. Often this is what makes someone aware they are a Receiver. As a Receiver they learn immediately:

- their loved one is close by and accessible, and

- communication will likely be energetic rather than physical.

The natural next step is to begin *sending* loving messages with confidence they are being received. The sense this will give of continuing relationship with a loved one beyond death can be deeply comforting and satisfying.

It requires only a little curiosity to get started as a Receiver.

THE MINDSET OF A "RECEIVER"

In the first week after Shera passed, I received contacts—actual messages—from Shera in the form of the poster and the little book, The way they were delivered literally *into my hands,* effectively made me a Receiver before I even knew it. (Chapter 5: A Letter from Heaven) They confirmed that Shera was close by, before the possibility of ongoing contact had even occurred to me; and before I even had a chance to integrate the unwanted "reality" that Shera was truly "gone" . . . and it left me expecting more.

Generally, it is the beliefs someone holds that are the most important factor in becoming a Receiver. It is deceptively simple: *You must believe that connecting with someone after death is possible, if it is to occur.* This necessary mindset can be learned. It can be nurtured and grown. It requires only a little curiosity to get started. (Chapter 13: Changing Beliefs)

CURIOSITY

Given the intensity of today's world, there is often little space to reflect on life and death, let alone what happens after death. For many people this will only happen when they are faced with the loss or imminent departure of a loved one. Then, when death has entered their life, it can dominate their attention in an instant, and their minds and emotions for days and months.

How strange then that we take such little time to consider death, let alone the impact it may have on our lives! So, it is no wonder when death shows up, many of us feel overwhelmed, confused, and disoriented.

It need not be this way. It's not hard to get information that can open our minds to other options. A single search word on the internet can lead to real people talking about personal experiences of a reality we have not been taught about and seldom think about—*and which they have lived*.

A single search word on the web can open doors to another world.

There are endless accounts of life before birth, and life after death, life *between* lives, and near-death experiences. They open doors to another world, a parallel world, that is intangible and unknown to many of us. This world has been revealed through regressions, hypnosis, dreams, dream analysis, and various kinds of energy work. There are many pathways to take, platforms that lead to fascinating new realms of thought: books, podcasts, YouTube and Netflix movies and documentaries, some of which share firsthand experiences of psychics, mediums, and hypnotherapists—and everyday people. In fact, if my experience can be taken as an example, some of the people you meet every day have stories they could tell of contact with, or messages from, departed loved ones—and they would be willing to share them if they were asked.

It was the occasional reading and viewing choices I had made over many years that had opened me to the spectrum of possibilities lying beyond the physical world. It had prepared me well for this time, and this new way of relating with Shera.

BODY VS SOUL

Earth to earth,

Ashes to ashes,

Dust to dust.

"From dust we come and to dust we shall return." Classic words spoken at a funeral. They have shaped the beliefs generations have held about death. Yet they address only a part of the truth.

These eloquent words relate only to the *body*. An integral part of becoming a Receiver, able to receive communication or connection "across the veil," is being able to believe, or at least accept the possibility, that:

- Each of us has a distinct body *and* Soul.
- The Soul carries one's life essence.
- The Soul survives death and continues on.

It is the body, not the Soul, that "returns to dust."

The first point was made clear to me in the moment of Shera's departure. It was in that instant I could see and feel that her body was utterly devoid of the *essence* of all that had been an integral part of my experience of this woman I had loved for so many years. Seeing it lying inert and lifeless, there was no doubt in my mind it had only *housed* her life essence, her vitality and personality. That life essence and vitality was no longer present.

"Dust to dust" only refers to what happens to the body. It is the body, not the Soul, that "returns to dust."

Yes, earth will be returned to earth, and dust to dust. However, this says nothing about what happens to the Soul essence that had transformed that "earth" and "dust," enlivening it to become the person and personality that was loved.

The body is the primary "evidence" of the Soul we love.

After all, what is this person we fall in love with? Think about it a moment. Despite Hollywood and all the glamour that comes with it, *Love* is not at first "sight." It goes deeper than that. There may indeed be great passion and a mutual adoration of beauty and body when lovers are first drawn together. However, decades later, when both the beauty and the young bodies are long gone, the love can still be there. In all likelihood, it will have grown even stronger.

The body is the primary "evidence" of the Soul we love and share life with. In other words, the "person" we love is essentially the *Spirit or Soul* "occupying" their body. Even as their body deteriorates with age to become at times unrecognizable from what it was, it continues undiminished.

The body is the primary evidence of the Soul we love.

BECOME AN OBSERVER

After returning from the crematorium with the ashes of Shera's body, at one point my lens shifted. I become aware of "observing" myself being in a state of grief and sadness. It was a subtle shift that made other things possible. (See Chapter 5: A Letters from Heaven)

And they happened in rapid succession. When I realized I couldn't bear staying locked in the pain, my focus shifted from *experiencing* it to knowing I had to *do* something—anything—to change the energy of that moment. In that instant, a part of me stepped *outside* my emotions. I had become an "Observer."

◆ ◆ ◆

Grief can block the channels needed for connection because it is often focussed on separation and loss. In my case, *by shifting my focus from grief, the connection I thought I had lost with Shera was almost instantaneously reestablished.*

Grief is an essential part of the healing process. Yet it was only when I became less identified with my loss, and "saw" my situation as untenable, that I was able to change the dynamic. I believe now, although I was unable to recognize or articulate it at the time, that I needed to learn to express my sadness *through feelings of love rather than grief.*

◆　◆　◆

THE TAKEAWAYS

❖ To be effective, a "Receiver" needs to cultivate a "habit of readiness" to receive them.

❖ Connection can come in ways that could never be anticipated.

❖ Love is built on the resonance we feel for someone's energy, personality, dreams, vitality and Soul essence—rather than on the appearance of their body.

❖ Although bodies are an essential component in any living relationship, death of the body need not mean the end of love nor the death of the relationship.

❖ To continue in relationship with a departed Soul, we must become more sensitive to energy.

Every day we miss messages sent from family, friends, and colleagues. Why? Because we didn't expect them, or we didn't know *when* their messages were going to come. Or we didn't know *what* they would look like (a letter? an email? a text message? a phone call?). Or we didn't know *how* they were coming (via the post office? an online browser? Facebook? WhatsApp? Telegram? Signal?).

Although in our physical realm we can easily list the ways messages might reach us from friends and colleagues, the possible channels through which they could come as *energy* from the other side are virtually unlimited.

CHAPTER 10

Where To Look

Once upon a time, a young girl was told she was going to receive some wonderful presents. Excited, the child sat by the front door with great anticipation, expecting at any moment to hear the sound of gifts being placed on the porch, dropped into the mailbox, or being put through the door slot. But nothing came. Day after day it was the same. Nothing arrived.

As time passed, the child's anticipation gradually turned into disappointment. The disappointment grew until she finally gave up hope the presents would ever arrive.

However, when the child turned around, she discovered the presents had indeed arrived! They had been there all along! They were piled up behind her! They had come in through the back doors, the side doors, and the windows. They had not been noticed because a simple assumption the child made unconsciously had turned all her attention in the wrong direction.

◆ ◆ ◆

There's something quite wonderful about how the brain works. It is like a dispatcher in a railway station managing trains as they arrive and depart. Ideally, the dispatcher has little to do because the whole system is fully automated. Everything runs automatically according to established schedules.

The brain is handling arriving nerve impulses. It develops systems—habits—so that any arriving stimulus will be dealt with efficiently, according to established "schedules," and sent on its way to where it needs to go. That's its job.

At a functional level, as far as your brain, the dispatcher, is concerned, the ideal situation is when everything is running automatically. At such times, it suspends its phenomenal analytical and monitoring capabilities, and just lets things continue on their own. That's how you can arrive at a shop, at work, or at home in your car without really having any recollection of how you got there. Your brain handled the trip automatically . . . by habit.

> ### "Belief" is a shorthand we use
> ### for a "habit" of thought.

However, when something unexpected happens, the brain instantly wakes up and goes into action. It searches past experiences and responses in search of an appropriate habit it can apply to whatever is currently happening. It analyzes the situation to determine whether it represents a risk or an opportunity.

This is the brain is working at its best. People experiencing this process feel energized, alert, and alive. As the brain works to develop an appropriate response, it is aware of things it would normally miss. Then, when the new situation is handled and done, the brain files the new response away for future reference—a new habit in the making—in case it ever becomes relevant again. Then, at the first opportunity it takes another "nap," so to speak, slipping back into automatic mode.

You may recognize this in your own life from the times you have found yourself in completely new and unfamiliar places, such as arriving at a new airport, visiting a new city, experiencing a different culture, or starting a new job. You tend to notice everything around you. This is because you are looking for anything you can recognize and use to navigate safely and effectively in the new situation.

IN A STRANGE NEW WORLD

There are parallels here to what someone may experience who has recently lost a loved one. They have effectively arrived in a strange new world, a world where their loved one is no longer present to receive their love. If they are losing someone with whom they have shared their life and dreams for many years, a vast, complex web of habits, sharing, loving, and connecting will have suddenly become irrelevant.

In this new situation, there is no "habit" for them to turn to or use. They are left without a program or structure they can recognize or fall back on. Everything is unfamiliar. It is no wonder they feel disoriented.

To have connection we need to develop new habits.

There are few guidelines to help navigate the emotions and changes they are dealing with. Socially, discussion of death and grief tends to be avoided altogether. This can lead to bouts of isolation and despair. As a result, it may not even occur to them that some kind of continuing after-death connection with their departed loved one may be possible.

For such a connection they need to develop new beliefs, and create new expectations; something their brains can turn to, and use in this "new world." (See Chapter 13: Beyond Beliefs) They need new habits.

In this and the following two chapters, I describe how it is possible to develop new the beliefs and expectations, that can lead to new habits.

◆　　◆　　◆

WHAT WAS IT EXACTLY THAT "DEPARTED," "LEFT," "PASSED ON?"

There is a story told in a poem of an Inuit woman who would go every year onto the tundra to rejuvenate her spirit. One year as she left on her annual pilgrimage, the people hearing her footsteps moving through the village, knew this time she would not return.

Three days later, a young man followed her tracks until he found her body where it was lying on the tundra beneath the broad Arctic sky.

The poem ends with the lines:

> *She had carried her tired old body as far as she could*
> *And then left it behind on the tundra.*

We often say "passed on" to avoid saying "died."

When someone has died, we often say they have "left their body." They "passed on." It is a way of avoiding the word "death," a topic which makes many people uncomfortable.

However, think about that for a moment: "Left their body." *What* was it that left their body? Yes, their body is still here . . . yet it is not the same. Clearly, as with the Inuit woman in the poem, *something* "left."

What "departed" is their personality, their humour, vision, and dreams—their vitality and their life force. All of these are what together comprised the experience of the "person" that was loved. They were part of the *energy*, the vital essence which had enlivened their body—and that "energy" was their *Spirit*.

The body they left behind was simply the vehicle through which their Spirit was able to live, function and express itself in a physical world.

Existing now as Spirit, they are no longer limited to the physical world. They exist as energy, unlimited by time and space. The customary ways of connecting with them and expressing love with gifts, dinners, nights out, touch, is no longer possible.

As energy, the departed loved one, now invisible, is using a new language of "energy," and it is that language that must be learned if we are to better understand and recognize their messages.

In order to contact someone in the spiritual world, there is some work to be done. A change of lenses may be in order as well, because we need to learn to *see* in a new way in order to notice things happening around us as expressions of energy.

In the rest of this chapter and the next, I explore ways to develop the habits that will help you recognize the signs that could be a departed loved one reaching out to you.

Relationship can continue beyond death.

A HABIT OF READINESS

Being "open to receive" means far more than sitting and waiting expectantly. Receiving is a very dynamic process. Perhaps the most effective way to maximize your ability as a Receiver of these "calls" from the other side, is to create a habit of anticipation—a readiness for connection. This will increase your sensitivity and make you more aware of what is happening around you. This increased awareness will facilitate connection that ultimately makes it possible for relationship to continue beyond death.

I was blessed when the first communication from Shera came not just as a "sign," but quite literally as a *message* delivered into my hands. (Chapter 5: Another Letter From Heaven) By proving to me we were still in "touch," this event put an end to the belief that she was gone, and created a new *belief* in me that she and I were still connected.

This belief created an *expectation* of more "connection" events. This became a *habit* which in turn helped me recognize subsequent signs and coincidences when they happened.

However, it is also possible for *unconscious* habits to get in the way. The child in the story at the start of this chapter had no trouble at all *believing* presents were coming. However, the habits built into her belief led her to expect the presents would come *in a particular way,* as they always had before. In other words, these assumptions became a barrier to the child's seeing what it was hoping for.

That is why it is also important to be aware of what beliefs you hold. A belief is a kind of shorthand the brain uses for a particular "habitual" way of thinking. Whenever we believe something, we subconsciously form an expectation of how it will "look," and that often becomes what we attune ourselves to watch for.

> ### *A belief is a kind of shorthand the brain uses for a particular "habitual" way of thinking.*

In this new kind of energy communication from a loved one on the other side, it's hard to know what to expect. However, because the one in spirit knows you and loves you, they know what will make sense to you. They can find ways to catch your attention. They are opportunistic and can be very creative, using whatever is at hand, and whatever energy may be moving in the moment, to create a sense of connections. I have provided many examples of this in Chapters 5, 6, and 7.

CREATIVE RECEPTIVITY

Because signs of connection can be very subtle, and "energy communicatins" can be unpredictable, it is necessary to work *consciously* to cultivate your sensitivity and imagination.

In the same way that *intending* to see a particular bird or plant, for example, will increase your chances of seeing them, this more dynamic state of expectation—of *creative* receptivity—will have the effect of opening and activating physical, emotional, mental, and spiritual "receptors."

In creating a state of "open readiness" as a Receiver, you will notice you are developing a greater awareness of what is around you, a finer sensitivity to details, *and flexibility both of focus and perspective.* It must be noted that once established, this elevated level of awareness, aside from maintaining relationship with a departed loved one, has benefits that will serve you in all areas of your life.

In my case, it has added a new dimension to the way I relate to everything in my environment, to the others around me, and to life itself. I am more able to see and appreciate the gifts that come to me every day, in ways I have never appreciated them before. My life has been enriched immeasurably.

They had both just accepted the separation was inevitable and had prepared themselves for it.

PLAN AHEAD

It can be a powerful and positive exercise to talk with your loved one about death *long before* death is even on the horizon . . . and also the possibility of having ongoing contact afterward. It will help you see each other through a different lens: as embodied Spirits living and expressing love together in a physical world. It's an opportunity to share thoughts with one another, set intentions, and make agreements.

When I shared these ideas with a woman I had just met, she totally agreed with me. "This was certainly true for me," she said." Then she went on to share this story:

A couple of years ago, my husband and I celebrated our thirty-sixth wedding anniversary. Aside from being a wonderful occasion, acknowledging all those years together, it also made both of us aware of our mortality.

We decided to talk about it . . . something we had never done before. We covered it all. We shared what our expectations were when we passed, what we wanted done with our bodies, and what kind of ceremony we would like to have. We even chose our gravestones.

She paused a second, and then continued:

My husband never got to celebrate our thirty-seventh anniversary.

She said in spite of the shock of his departure coming so soon and being so unexpected, she had been so much better able to handle it. They had both just accepted that separation was inevitable, and had prepared themselves for it. She could sense his presence in everything, hearing his voice, so to speak, in all the decisions that were made. This made the pain and grief she felt so much less than it otherwise would have been.

◆　　◆　　◆

The beliefs you may currently hold can be addressed and modified. Yet, even if you and your loved one hold different belief systems, when the separation comes, having had a conversation together may increase the chance you will recognize signs when they appear.

Current beliefs can be modified.

When we lived on Galiano Island we had a neighbour whose husband passed away several months before Shera. She was also an artist, a dynamic, individual who was very engaging, and comfortable with her emotions. She loved nature and was sensitive to the energies around her in the garden and the forest. She fully believed people have souls, that there is life after death, and the Soul continues on.

Her husband was also a sensitive and loving person. However, he was a scientist, a rational thinker. He would only accept as true, something that had been "proven," reviewed, and if possible, reported in published studies. As a result, in his belief, "souls" were just an engaging fantasy. He was convinced death was final. "When you die, that's it. There is no more."

Although Anne believed connection was possible after death, and wanted to open the possibility of connection with him after he left, she knew she would never change his mind. At some point in their discussions, she came up with a suggestion. "Okay. Look, if you get there and discover that you are still here, send me a message of some kind."

She had said "if." With that condition, he was able to agree. She suggested he send a yellow bird.

Communication from a departed loved one always carries meaning or significance for the Receiver.

Days after he passed, she went up to the study they had shared. She had not been near his desk since he left and was intrigued to discover the lower drawer in his desk was open. She noticed one folder sitting higher than the others. She lifted it out to look at it. To her great surprise and delight she discovered it was a file he had kept of the love letters they had exchanged over the years. A sign? Perhaps.

In any case it was a welcome surprise. She sensed his presence. Then, later in the day, as she was walking across the garden, a yellow bird, flying low, passed directly above her head and on into the forest. Typically, on Galiano, yellow birds are rarely if ever seen.

WHAT CHANNELS DO SPIRITS USE?

Contact from a departed loved one who exists as an *energy* being in the spiritual realm, will likely be quite different from communication we would normally expect in our physical world. To further complicate things, there is no "one way" contacts are made. As I shared earlier, the "messages" I have received from Shera over the months and years since she left have come in dozens of different ways and forms, many of which I could never have expected. That being said, there is one cardinal principle to understand: *any communication from a departed loved one always has meaning or significance for the Receiver.* In the following chapter, I share how to separate the messages from the background noise.

ENERGY

So, what does it mean to say that messages may come as "energy?" What does that look like? Energy is non-linear, non-directional, non-physical, and invisible.

> ### *Energy is non-linear, non-directional, non-physical, and invisible.*

I imagine in the same way our creativity fires up when we are faced with a task that challenges our limits, loved ones in spirit rise to the challenge of sending messages to loved ones in the physical realm. In my case, I have found their creativity can be beyond amazing. Stories I shared in earlier chapters will already have given you a sense of how inventive they can be. They can also demonstrate a healthy sense of humour! An example of this was when Shera sent Nick, who was a figurative author "clone" of myself, to ensure I got the point I had missed in an earlier message. (Chapter 7: A Dear Unfinished Task)

Messages can be known and identified by their impact and effects. They are often associated with colours, movements, objects, action, and momentum. They may manifest as particular sounds: an eagle's cry, a signature tune, a favourite song being played at the perfect time. There may be an unexpected notification on your cell phone, or website link or video, a flickering or drop of signal, an interruption of power. Anything operating with electricity, microwaves or light, by brightening, behaving erratically, turning on, or shutting down can become a means through which people in spirit may deliver signs and signals energetically.

There are three modes or "channels" through which "energy" communications from Spirit may arrive:

◆ External

◆ Internal

◆ Nature

EXTERNAL CHANNELS

Many times, messages are carried in the *association* that one has with particular objects which appear unexpectedly. Rather than lifting and carrying physical objects, spirits usually act on physical objects indirectly, *influencing* them so they play out or behave unexpectedly. Questions arise: "How did that happen?" "How did that get here?"

Energy influences objects in state of change or flux.

Deidre, a visitor to the gallery, told me that shortly after her mother passed away, she had gone out to an event where she bought a ticket to a raffle. Later, when the winning numbers were drawn, she found she was holding the winning ticket. The prize turned out to be a bottle of "Joy" perfume. She was delighted. "That was my mother's favourite perfume!" Evidently to make sure she got the message, she also won second prize—another bottle of Joy perfume. Now, years later, she says, "one of the bottles still sits on my dresser."

Energy is best able to influence a physical object when it is in a state of instability or flux, for example:

◆ When the object is falling or turning, as in the ball in a raffle or lottery, or a set of dice. (Chapter 5: Word Play)

◆ When cards are being shuffled and drawn. (Chapter 5: Word Play) Tarot, I Ching and other "oracles" are examples of this.

◆ In the movement of the wind and the flow of water, and in the play of light and shadows. An example of this is when an eagle's shadow passed over me as I was talking with a friend by the gallery about where I would place Shera's ashes. (Chapter 5: Eagles)

◆ During times of transition—sunrise and sunset, or waking up and going to sleep. For example, after I asked my goddaughter what Shera's gift was to the world, it was only when I was waking up the next morning that I "got the message": Shera had answered our question using the words in her word bowl, "Joy, joy inside." (Chapter 5: A Letter from Heaven)

◆ When something catches your attention as you are looking through pages of a directory, or conducting an online search, scrolling through a play list, or viewing Facebook posts or YouTube videos.

Messages may be delivered by people who may not even be aware they are acting as messengers.

Clearly, given certain circumstances just about anything can embody a message: a book, a letter, a note, a post, a piece of music, a flower, a gift. It may not even be an "object" as such, but rather a particular shape or a shadow—any of these may be creatively and energetically "purposed" by a Spirit on the other side.

Messengers

Remarkably, messages can literally be *delivered* by people who may not even be aware they are acting as messengers. I have shared several examples of this. When Sharon delivered Carol's message to Matt, she knew she was the messenger, deliberately passing on the message.

(Chapter 8: Open to Receive) However, when Marilyn, the new tenant downstairs, said "Read this!" and put a small book written by Shera into my hand, she had no idea she had been made a messenger (Chapter 5: Another Letter from Heaven) Once I had a message delivered by *two* friends. First Shera put the thought into a friend's head to send me a poem. Although I recognized it was a message from her, I had missed an important part of it. So, later, she later sent another messenger, Nick, to spell out clearly for me the part that I had missed (Chapter 7: A Dear Unfinished Task)

INTERNAL CHANNELS

Although the dramatic effect of seeing a message manifesting phys-ically in objects around you can be compelling, contact from the other side can also be established in more subtle ways as well. After all, we are talking about messages being sent from departed loved ones who are now spirits, energy beings, living in a non-physical realm. It seems logical they would seek to connect with us more often through the manipulation of energy than through something physical with weight and mass. To receive such messages, we need to become more aware of what is happening within our minds and bodies.

When you change the way you see things
The things you are looking at will change.

Thoughts and Ideas

Although we are all bound in a three-dimensional, physical reality, the vast majority of us are largely ignorant of our internal emotional and physical dynamics. Instead, we tend to spend our days, 24/7, focussed largely on what we must deal with in an external material world. Unless something is causing pain or discomfort, we are generally unaware of what is happening in our bodies. It is no wonder, then, out of habit, when we are looking for messages and contact, we tend look for them outside our bodies, even though internal signs can be much more profound and immediate.

Imagine for example, some moment in the day, when out of the clear blue a thought or picture of your loved one comes to mind . . . a memory perhaps. Or you suddenly have an insight or an "Aha!" moment. Yet it is completely out of context in that moment and does not relate to what you may be dealing with. Why did that happen?

Have you ever said, "I have no idea where that thought came from"? A more intriguing question would be, "Was that thought even *mine?*"

Because a thought, memory, or dream is an energy phenomenon, it may have been the work of the spirit of a departed loved one reaching out, as Christa reached out to Sharon. (Chapter 9: Open to Receive) In my case, several times when I have faced a challenge in the writing of this book, I was awakened in the middle of the night, a solution clearly in mind, feeling compelled to write it down.

The presence of a departed loved one or Spirit can be signalled by a sudden unexplainable physical sensation.

Intuition

Energy messages do not necessarily come through the mind. They may arrive more as a sensation: a "gut feeling," for example, or an unexpected thought, a "just knowing," a "sense" of certainty.

We often take actions, choose things, or make decisions on the basis of such sensations, and are pleased when we discover we had indeed made the right choice. In our conversations we commonly attribute those things which positively influence our lives to good luck or to chance, or to higher guidance, angels, or God. Whether we are aware of it or not, these are all ways of acknowledging *energy beings* and the role they can play in guiding us.

It is not a great stretch then, to reflect in certain circumstances, on whether these energy sensations may be an intervention by a departed loved one who. They have just become, after all, a recently arrived "energy being." Some people even consider a departed loved one as a personal guardian angel.

Dreams

In addition to being delivered as a thought, an idea, or a memory, messages can also come in the form of daytime, sleeping, or lucid dreams. A dramatic example of this is described in the story Sharon shared of the visits she received from Christa. (Chapter 8: Matt and Christa)

The Senses

Intangible messages can be detected by physical sensations.

Paradoxically, some "intangible," i.e., non-physical, energy messages, *can* indeed be detected with your physical senses. Many have reported "sensing" the presence of a departed loved one or spirit as a sudden unexplainable *physical* sensation:

- A sudden feeling of warmth or cold
- Feeling a breeze when the air is still
- Feeling a pressure somewhere on the body
- Goose bumps on the arm or hair "standing on end" on the back of the neck
- A vibration, a feeling of electricity
- A familiar "trademark" scent or taste
- A sound of a voice, or music no one else hears

NATURE'S CHANNELS

Nature is another non-physical channel through which messages may be sent to us. This may sound at first like a contradiction. After all, isn't nature physical? Trees, mountains, lakes, and oceans? That certainly is true. However, pause a moment and change the lens you are using. Think of what you do when you are feeling depleted or exhausted, in low energy? Or when pressures of the day leave you stressed and depressed, and feeling "down?"

It would be no surprise to hear you make a point of getting out to sit in a park, walk in a forest, or on a mountain trail, by a river, or spending time on a lake, or an oceanside beach—*somewhere in nature*. Why is that? It's not just the physical elements of nature that draw you there. You have only to think of how you feel after going there: relieved, expanded . . . *recharged*. It's the *energy* you receive, the rejuvenation you feel. You've "recharged" your batteries.

> ### *Departed loved ones can send messages through an infinite variety of channels.*

Once you leave the city, roads, and highways to spend time in nature, you are stepping into a dynamic interplay of energies: sky and earth, plants and animals, Earth and life in all its forms. Nature is a vast charging station. You can *feel* it filling you up again, charging you with energy any time you give it a chance.

That is why it is no surprise departed loved ones, existing now as energy themselves, can send messages through any of the infinite variety of energy channels available in nature. I have described many of them in earlier chapters:

- ◆ Animals (eagles, ravens, Canada Geese) (Chapter 5: Beyond Words Nature Speaks)
- ◆ Light (eagle shadow) (Chapter 5: Eagles)

- Sun and weather (Sun breaks through clouds) (Chapter 5: Eagles)
- Time of day (Chapter 7: A Dear Unfinished Task)

Symbols

From the earliest days when humans evoked the power of animals in paintings on the walls of caves, and carved them into stones, the spiritual energies of animals have been universally recognized around the world.

In many shamanic cultures, individuals may be endowed with the intrinsic strengths and characteristics of a particular animal. This is known as their totem animal. Entire clans may be named for particular animals in the belief the energy, the essence, and characteristics of the totem animal is manifested in each person of the clan and the clan as a whole.

Animals have always carried symbolic meanings and significance.

The strengths and attributes of animal energy have become enshrined in our language.

- "Wise as an owl."
- "Smart as a fox."
- "Busy as a bee."
- "Stubborn as a mule."
- "Strong as an ox."

It was only after Shera passed that I begin to realize the role nature and animals would play in our ongoing connection. As I reported in Chapter 5: Nature Speaks, I have found tremendous value in the unexpected arrival or behaviour of an animal or bird that has caught my attention at a time when, "coincidentally," I was engaged with thoughts of Shera.

After such an event, I found it to be well worthwhile to check one of the many websites offering "spiritual" profiles and "symbolic" meanings of the animals. This change of lenses let me tap into the centuries old wisdom of other cultures, and invariably gave me valuable insights.

◆　◆　◆

Once you have a sense of the general channels through which messages may come to you, another question immediately arises: *"How can you better recognize a "sign" as a message when it happens?"*

◆　◆　◆

THE TAKEAWAYS

❖ Grief and the intensity of grief we feel is directly influenced by what we believe.

❖ We increase chances of getting messages if we create a habit of open readiness to receive them.

❖ Messages and signs can be physical, energetic or symbolic.

❖ Messages can be experienced internally as body sensations, thoughts, and feelings.

It is not uncommon for most of us to encounter people who were born and grew up in other countries. For the most part, we are able to meet and develop a relationship with them *only* because they have taken the time to make the effort to learn *our* language.

It follows then that the reverse is true: if we want to build a relationship with someone who does *not* speak our language, it will help if we were to learn some of the "language" they are using.

In doing so, we would also learn new ideas, new perspectives and potentially a new way of seeing—and *being*—in the world.

CHAPTER 11

Recognizing The Signs

With Shera's passing I was offered a different lens which suddenly let me gaze into a Reality so vast it cannot be comprehended. It was rare opportunity to explore more deeply into the Mystery. To feel it in a way that had evaded me in my normal life. It gave rise to questions that carried ms beyond the usual narrow boundaries of my life and days.

◆   ◆   ◆

Once I understood how different "channels" could be used through which energy initiated in the non-physical realm could enter into the physical world, I was able to "see" more. I found myself wondering how I recognized when something was a "communication," and how I could be sure such signs were indeed messages from Shera.

MEDIUMS

There are people who are able to see (*clairvoyant*) and hear (*clairaudient*) directly with those who have passed on and exist now in spirit. They are called "mediums." A session with an experienced, qualified medium can offer a comforting reassurance for anyone desiring to know "for sure" that their loved have not "died;" that they continue to exist and indeed are capable of communicating.

In a single session with a medium, even those who may not believe such things are possible can quickly become believers when the medium gives them information known *only* to them and the one who has moved on. Finding this kind of information is fundamental to "evidential mediumship" and is a priority for every reliable medium. This is how it becomes possible to verify the identification of the spirit they have contacted.

A single session with a medium can make a doubter believe.

There are countless stories illustrating this . . . quiet accounts of people connecting with relatives. For example:

"There is an older woman here, she may be your grandmother." A medium is speaking to her client, a woman in her thirties.

After a pause she adds, "She's showing me an orange cushion. She likes the orange cushion." "Does that mean anything to you?"

The woman is surprised . . . almost speechless. "Why, yes! Orange was my grandmother's favourite colour. Just two days ago, I bought an orange cushion in honour of her, and I put it on her favourite chair!"

Given one session like this and you will *know* that your loved one is still around, that they love you, and that they are wanting to be in connection with you.

◆　◆　◆

I have been aware of mediums for a long time. Indeed, the idea remained an engaging fantasy until a succession of books, reports, and compelling documentaries, easily available online, led me to believe it was true. Some highly attuned mediums like James van Praag, Susan Giesemann, and Nancy Orlen Weber, describe remarkable instances in which they received verifiable information *no living person could know*. Information which could only be known by a departed Soul. In some accounts, they have helped police solve cases with information that could only be known by the person who passed away.

> **To believe only mediums can connect with departed Souls is a way of saying "Other people can—not me."**

I was unaware, however, that as I came to believe mediums could establish a connection with people on the other side, I was also forming a belief that *only* mediums could connect with departed Souls and receive messages directly.

This was disempowering myself. It was a way of saying *"Other people can—not me."* It is self-limiting and could quickly become a self-fulfilling belief, an automatic way of thinking—a habit. After all, once you have dismissed any possibility you could receive messages from the other side, then you will likely discount any "signals" you get energetically—and yet they may be the very connection you have wanted with the departed Soul,

It is true that mediums *may be* able to "see" and "hear" things being shown and spoken to them by a visiting spirit. Yet the majority of the time, as in the story above with the orange cushion, they are merely *reporting* on those sensations they sense or experience, see, or hear. They do not necessarily know their meaning or whether they have significance.

For example, at one point a medium I was with told me, "Shera is showing me a candle. Is someone having a birthday?" When I replied. "No," she asked when my birthday was. Even though it had been two months earlier, she said, "I think she is wishing you a happy birthday."

I laughed, "No. That's not what she is doing!" and I told her the story about the surprise birthday cake, and how the candles had gone out spontaneously, only to reignite all at once a moment later. (Chapter 5: Play)

Then it was her turn to laugh. "Well *that* explains it! When I came down to make this call, I suddenly got the idea to light some candles." She turned the laptop so I could see the three candles burning beside her.

"It was strange because normally I don't burn candles in my sessions with people."

She went on, "But then a thought came to mind that was even more strange. I thought of doing an advanced exercise with the psychic class I will be teaching this afternoon. It was something I did when I was learning."

I was intrigued.

Mediums do not necessarily understand the information they receive.

She went on to explain, "We would form a circle around a burning candle and together we would focus on extinguishing it—*psychically.*" Then she added "Shera was definitely working with me before this call!" and she laughed again.

It was on this call that I remembered Shera and I had *always* created a surprise for each others' birthdays, and to my delight, two years after the event, I realized she had managed to "surprise" me yet again, on the first birthday I had after she passed! Clearly, wherever she was, Shera wanted to make sure I knew she was the one behind the candles going out and then reigniting. I could almost hear her laughing in delight."

Mediums do not necessarily understand the *significance* or meaning of the information they receive, because it often comes as images, symbols, or obscure references. It is in a kind of "code" so to speak. The key to breaking that code is held by the people with whom the medium is working. After all they are the ones the spirit is wanting to reach.

That is when the symbols or "information" become a *"message."*

Becoming aware of this is very empowering for a Receiver. Then the question is, "How does one *recognize* a message among all the things that are happening in any given moment?"

EXTRASENSORY PERCEPTION

We are taught the classical five senses of seeing, hearing, feeling, tasting, and smelling are ways our bodies monitor and inform us about the *physical* world around us. "Extrasensory perception," often called a "sixth sense," refers to *non*-physical experiences that cannot be explained in terms of the normal five senses. It describes ways in which we experience *energy*.

You are constantly receiving extrasensory information.

The love you feel spontaneously at times for a departed loved one may be a response to love they are sending you.

It's no surprise then that extrasensory perception is one of the most important tools for a Receiver wanting to receive messages from energy beings in the energy realm. Whether you are aware of it or not, your extrasensory "receptors" are constantly receiving information from the energy field around you.

This kind of sensing can be experienced as a hunch, an intuition, a gut feeling, a "just knowing," or a premonition. *Knowing* something was going happen, for example, before it does, or thinking of a friend just before they call or arrive for a visit. Telepathy, precognition, clairvoyance, and clairaudience are all forms of extrasensory experience.

Even if science is hard pressed to explain these things, there is nothing controversial here. In spite of general social conditioning not to notice or give weight to such things, extrasensory perception is a natural part of being human. Not only do each of us have our own experiences of it, some people even consciously guide their life decisions by it.

You could experience this in various ways. It could be a time when your deceased loved one unexpectedly comes to mind. It could be your extrasensory awareness picking up on their "presence," letting you know they're not so far away. It could be a response to the love coming *from them*. This is no different from times when you think of a friend just before they call you or arrive for a visit.

People who have had near-death experiences routinely report the angels and people they met during the time they were on the other side communicated with them telepathically. Isn't it only natural, then, to suppose a sudden thought about a departed loved one, which is completely out of context with what you are doing, could have been initiated from the other side? It could be a spontaneous memory, or a feeling of love for them that just happens to come to your awareness. That's how energy works. There is no time. There is no distance.

When you find yourself in sustained grief or despair, they will be feeling it on the other side.

If energy moves in both the physical and energetic realms, and telepathy is the "language" of energy, then it would likely cross from realm to realm in either direction. Any time you are feeling love for your loved one, wishing you could hug them or hold them and send your love to them, *they will have already received it.*

However, this would also mean that when you are feeling the pain of their absence, they are also aware of that. They might even feel distress if you are in sustained grief or despair, as Christa was with Matt. (Chapter 8: Opening a Channel)

This kind of telepathic link could is shown in the story of a woman in Mexico who lost her family, her husband and two children, in a devastating accident. The tragedy had come at a time when they had all been engaged in a project they had dedicated themselves to as a family. It had not been completed, and now risked having to be abandoned altogether.

In spite of feeling bereft and very alone, as the only one of the "team" who survived, the woman still had a strong motivation to complete the project that they had begun together.

This awakened in her the desire of connecting with them, and remarkably, she set her intention to do just that. In time she became more and more aware of them and their presence until she reached a point where she felt they had become a part of all her days. After a time, she could say without hesitation or doubt, "My children have saved me or protected me from a lot of accidents and from people who were no good or may be intending harm to me."

Love* is *the medium, and it reaches beyond time and space.

She said, "This is something that people can awaken in themselves," and added, "You only have to choose."

All energy is part of a vast, limitless energy field encompassing and comprising all things. Love is energy. You do not have to be a "medium" to get—or to give—a loving energy "message." Love *is* the medium, and it reaches beyond time and space.

HOW TO BECOME SENSITIVE TO THE SIGNS

If we are to accept the premise here of non-physical largely replacing the physical modes of communication and the importance of extrasensory perception, where does a Receiver begin to develop the sensitivity needed to recognize contact and receive messages? In the current world, particularly in the West, life is generally experienced as a nuts and bolts, left-brain, largely materialistic, science-oriented, physical world. We are informed not just by the classic five senses, first named by Aristotle over 2,300 years ago, but by between twenty to thirty additional senses recognized by scientists in the centuries since: senses such as the senses of balance, thirst, pressure, proprioception, and heat, along with many others.

When any one of these senses draws your attention, your perception of the world will shift, becoming sharper in the area of the awakened sense. There have been many studies that illustrate this.

In one, participants are spontaneously asked to look around for about half a minute or so, letting their eyes scan everything in the space around them. Then they were asked—without looking again—to write down everything they noticed in the room, that had the colour red in it.

When they were done, they were asked to look around the space again.

In developing your ability to receive, you will also be expanding the boundaries of your world.

Invariably, the second time they *noticed* many more things with red in them. They had been made *sensitive* to red, and as a result saw it in more places.

◆　　◆　　◆

Perception is more than the simple sum of the information coming from our senses. It shifts according to different "filters." As this exercise showed, you can choose which filters to put in place in order to become more sensitive to particular things. What you "perceive" is what you become conscious of *after* information has passed through at least these three filters:

- ◆ Your attention—this is where you can consciously direct your perception
- ◆ Your beliefs—the dominant controller of perception
- ◆ Your expectations—which are often born out of your beliefs

When you set an intention to be more sensitive to subtle signs, you will begin to notice them more and more. In time, this will strengthen your perception, which in turn will improve your ability as a Receiver.

There is a bonus to all of this, as well. By developing your ability to receive both sensory and extrasensory signs, you will naturally become a more sensitive and conscious observer, much more aware of what is happening in every moment, as life unfolds around you. This means the boundaries of your world will be expanding to include information and gifts beyond anything you can now imagine.

Becoming a more sensitive and conscious observer will expand the boundaries of your world.

BUILDING THE SKILLS OF DISCERNMENT

"Looking" is a general function. It is automatic. It happens because your eyes are open. If it is not focussed or directed at anything, it may not pick up on anything in particular. It is like the scanning you did in the exercise above.

It is only when something stands out from the background noise that you "see" it. Seeing only requires a minimal level of attention and focus. Often, we do not move beyond that.

Three skills will help elevate your sensitivity beyond this fundamental scanning level so you will be more likely to perceive more around you, and better able to *discern* a connection with a departed loved one when it comes.

Simply stated, the process consists of increasing your capacity to:

◆ *Realize* what you are looking at.

◆ *Recognize* its context.

◆ *Reflect* on its gifts.

Realize—Become Aware

Something catches your attention. That is, you have become conscious of it. As you turn your attention to it, you become aware of its form, size, patterns, colours, and textures.

To grow the skill of awareness, develop the habit of consciously noticing and looking again whenever something catches your eye. To illustrate this, think of the classic "double take" in a comedy. A kind of "Did I actually see that?" reflex. Then subtle things become clearer. Instead of dismissing coincidences, you will be training yourself *to become aware of them.*

In my case, for example, when I returned from the crematorium with Shera's ashes (Chapter 5: A Letter from Heaven) and needed to get out of the pain I was feeling, I *looked* around the room and *saw* the small dresser with the papers piled on top of it. As I moved the papers, I became aware of the large poster as something I had not seen at first and did not expect. I did a double-take. I became curious about how I could have missed it. I picked it up and turned it over.

Identification is the first step in discovering that something may be a sign or message.

Recognize and Identify Context

This is the job of your left brain, which labels and documents the tangible, measurable world for you. This process of identification and naming the elements of an event—*and* recognizing their context, the order of events, and location--is the first step in discovering the possibility that something which has been noticed may be a sign or carry a message.

To grow this ability, you need to become more aware, more conscious of where you are, what you are doing, what is happening around you and the flow of events.

In my example, of course, while holding the poster in my hands, I recognized the photo and how the joyfulness of it brought me to laughter, changing my mood in an instant.

Reflect

This is when your right brain becomes engaged, subliminally at first, and more consciously later. As you identify the elements of what you have seen and noticed, you become more conscious; more aware of things *beyond* what you are actually looking at: emotion, symbols, and the interrelationship and timing of an event. You make assessments at a subconscious level. You become aware of the relevance of an event, how it coincides with other things, and your emotional response to it. You notice the timeliness or synchrony of it.

> **Simply reviewing the events of a day may lead you to notice things you hadn't noticed at the time they happened.**

To grow this skill, you need to develop the ability to look beyond what *is happening to discover the broader context of it. That means how it relates to the things around it, its timing, and what you were thinking and feeling at the time.*

In my case, in reading the poem on the poster I spontaneously related it to my having asked Shera to send me a sign now and then to let me know how she was doing and that she was okay. I also noticed the synchronicity of its arrival at the time I was in my deepest grief.

To work with reflection, develop the habit of revisiting events that have caught your attention. Simply reviewing the events of a day may lead you to notice things you hadn't noticed at the time. Consider the elements and details, and relate them to time of day, what you were feeling, the location, what happened before and what came after, and what else was happening at the same time.

REFLECTION

While the first two skills are skills of perception applied in the moment, reflection is perhaps the most powerful key to unlocking the deeper dimensions of an event. It can be employed at any time. The right brain in particular, continues to work with and review events, as in a dream, especially those with an emotional component. Even long after the event is completed and over, taking a moment for reflection may make you aware of additional factors, perhaps an unsuspected implication which could lead you to an "Aha!" moment. This is what can validate the likelihood that you had been given a sign or message.

> ### Reflection is the key to unlocking
> ### deeper dimensions of an event.

Reflection can happen at any time. It may take the form of a dream or the discovery of another related event or fact that wasn't known at the time. It can be the recognition of an unfolding pattern that only becomes evident after time has passed. I describe how that happened for me in Chapter 7 when, upon reflection, I realized seemingly random and unrelated *events* over a period of months had been consistent with an overall *pattern* that was advancing me in my life and aligning me with my purpose.

In another example, two years after the poster suddenly appeared on the day of the cremation to help me realize Shera had not "gone," I was reflecting again on the poster. I noticed in the photo she was standing in front of a large painting. Although I had *looked* at this image dozens of times, this was something I had not *seen*. When I finally *saw* it, I *noticed* the two hearts and *identified* it as the painting Shera created to celebrate our relationship. This even further strengthened the message I had taken from the event that we were still in relationship. (See page 8)

MORE ON REFLECTION

Reflection leads to insight and discovery. It offers a change of lenses and different perspectives that can add depth and clarity to an event. We may call it good luck or bad luck at the time. However, we don't know if it's important or not. We can't evaluate whether something has critical significance, or how it will ultimately impact our life, until it has been played out and we can reflect on it in the context of the passage of time,

Reflection can reveal the essence of the
Soul of the one we love.

It is upon reflection that the symbolic dimensions of an event may be recognized. This happened for me, for example, soon after Shara had passed when a pair of Canada geese changed course at the instant I saw them, and flew *directly* toward me to land at the water's edge only a few meters in front of me. When I checked on the spiritual significance of Canada geese, I found that they represent loyalty and steadfastness of relationship. I learned they form lifelong pairs. One does not leave its mate behind.

This discovery was very comforting, and at the time I was easily able to take it as a "message" reassuring me that Shera had not left me. (Chapter 5: Geese)

Reflection is perhaps most important for the role it can play in revealing to us essences of the Soul that has passed, their passions and concerns, their dreams and their purpose—and the love and relationship shared.

◆　　◆　　◆

THE TAKEAWAYS

❖ A communication is for you; therefore often only you will know if a sign or event is a "mesage."

❖ Because a departed Soul is in an energy realm and works with energy, we must focus less on the physical and become sensitive to communications arriving through some form of energy.

❖ Maintaining an attitude of open-minded attentiveness increases the ability receive messages.

❖ Because messages come in an infinite variety of forms, it is important to be conscious at all times of what is unfolding around you.

❖ To be an effective Receiver, it is important to know what your beliefs are, what your expectations are, and where you put your attention.

❖ Taking time to reflect on an event is the most important tool in discovering its deeper significance.

We arrived as newborns into a physical world that was unfamiliar to us. Yet we quickly learned to recognize what we found around us. We learned to interact with people and how to work with things.

Similarly, after someone we love passes on, when we seek connection with them, we are putting ourselves once again on the threshold of a world that is unfamiliar to us—a non-physical world of energies and higher frequencies.

Yet here too, we can quickly learn to recognize the different forms and shapes energy can take around us. We can learn to understand it and work with it to interact with Souls that have gone ahead.

CHAPTER 12

Confirming It's Real

We have no idea how many levels of the Game of Life are playing out around us at any given time.

◆   ◆   ◆

In the beginning, I was unsure how to share with others outside of my household about this time, and the remarkable things I was experiencing. I was just trying to understand it myself! I also needed to reassure myself that what I was considering to be a "sign" or message was not simply wishful thinking.

But where could I look for that reassurance? Particularly when, if these events *were* signs or messages of some kind, they would be intended only for the person being contacted—me—and therefore delivered in terms often only I could recognize and understand.

As much as I may have wished for connection with Shera and was captivated by these events, I also needed to be reassured that a supposed connection was "real." That it was not just imagined. Possibly I was fooling myself. That is one reason why it has been gratifying to find that virtually any time I have spoken of my experiences with someone, they have responded with their own story of contact with a loved one who has passed on. I hear the delight in their words and see it glowing in their faces. That is how I came to believe love continues beyond death and beyond grief.

Yet who can confirm a particular, apparently random, event is a "communication" of some kind? The first hint is in the question itself: that such a question should be raised about *one particular event* among countless "events" occurring simultaneously in every moment all the time. The person raising the question is the one who noticed it might be a "message." Even if others are present at the time, that person is usually the *only* person who noticed it; therefore, the only one in whom the question arises. Invariably, that is also the person for whom the communication was intended *and who is, therefore, the only person who could decode it*. In my case that person was *me*.

The only person for whom the communication was intended is the only one who can "decode" it.

A PARADOX

Tools normally used in the physical world as a way of "proving" an experience are generally not applicable when that experience is energetic and emotional. How can you find "objective" proof in something that is in many ways a totally "subjective" experience or interpretation of an event?

For example, how can I know that one of countless random happenings in any given day carries a "message?" There are too many unanswered and unanswerable questions. This I believe is one of the reasons people are reluctant to share their stories of such things. "Proving" to others what is—even if true—essentially a "private" communication, and probably one they would not understand anyway, is somewhat pointless.

There was a period in the writing of this book when everything had become laborious for me. I was attempting at some subtle level to "prove" rather than simply "share" my experience. Once I realized this, I decided to drop what was an impossible burden of proof. Instead, I developed several principles—lenses I could train on events to test whether what I was experiencing was credible as a connection or not.

MAKE COINCIDENCE YOUR TOUCHSTONE

In our modern age, "coincidence" has been given a bad rap. It is a social outcast. It has become the "go to" word for someone who wants to dismiss anything they do not personally believe, or which makes them uncomfortable.

Coincidences are the most important piece of evidence.

Yet this hasn't always been the case. It could be argued our whole body of human knowledge, whether scientific, esoteric, or shamanic has been founded on coincidence, the observation and recognition of coincidences. The co-*incidence* of events. Something coming together with, or happening with, something else—without evident connection or cause. It is unfortunate a word with such a proud history has become a label for derision.

Coincidences are the key piece of evidence. They are not to be dismissed in any context. In using this word to dismiss what we cannot immediately believe, we shut down our ability to properly assess important elements of events around us, or to discover the relationship between them.

For shamans and scientists alike, the main tool of insight has been recognition of coincidence. The specific, observed reality of how elements coincide in time and space is the basis of discovery. It lies behind the "Aha!" moment . . . the shout of "Eureka!"

Coincidences present mysteries to be solved. They invite us to find the interrelationship of the elements that came together in coincidental phenomena. This must come before any attempt to determine cause of an event.

This becomes particularly pertinent in considering communication with departed people and spirits on the other side. *The ability to recognize a coincidence occurring in a context which gives it meaning or significance, is the most important skill for a Receiver.*

"Synchronicity" is the word that was created by Carl Jung to refer to events which gain *meaning* because they are associated with a coincidence. There is nothing particularly unique or special about seeing a bird, a falling leaf, or a burst of sunlight. All day long we receive online posts, memes, and video clips. These kinds of things are happening around us all the time. What makes a particular one of them a possible "message," a sign, or a symbol is that it can appear to gain *meaning* in the context of what is happening around it—coincident with it—*and the fact that it appears at the perfect time.*

For shamans and scientists alike, coincidence has been the first tool of insight.

Synchronicity addresses one critical aspect of coincidence: the *significance* of events occurring simultaneously, without any clearly identifiable cause or obvious link. For example, it was a coincidence, *co-incidental,* that I drew a "Joy" card *while in a discussion about the gift Shera brought to the world.* It became more remarkable when the coincidence happened not just once but twice. (Chapter 5: Word Play) What made this event so extraordinary was the degree of significance the cards gained because they carried the word that was Shera's "brand."

Although we are talking here about coincidence and synchronicity in the context of communication with the Spirit Realm, they are happening around us all the time. Once we become fully aware of this, the world ceases to be "normal" in the common sense of the word. It becomes magical . . . a doorway to the super-natural.

It also becomes a teacher. First Nations people, bushmen of the Kalahari, shamans, and aboriginals around the world have known this since the beginning of time. You don't have to go far to find telltales of this in all cultures. Coincidence and synchronicity are fundamental to the practices of tarot, astrology, numerology, and all other oracles and arts of divination.

If you are reading this discussion using the lens of our so-called "real" world, with its day-to-day assumptions, habits, and conventions, you may find it a stretch to take in some of the information and ideas presented here. If so, consider this: for almost a century, the leading edge of science has explored unique interrelationships they could observe at increasingly sub-atomic levels. This work has led us to the point today where coincidence and synchronicity are no longer seen by many leading scientists as "accidents," but rather uniquely observable evidence, if not actual proof, of how *everything* is inter-linked and entangled in a vast unified field of energy—the "quantum field."

Coincidence and synchronicity are no longer seen as "accidents," but rather uniquely observable evidence.

This discovery is one of the many gifts that can come to us organically as our attention is drawn into the Mystery that accompanies death. If there are no mistakes in the world, then a coincidence which has come into your life carries significance, in a sense, *because* you have noticed it. Why? *As the one noticing it—as the Receiver—you are a part of it.*

Beyond developing your skills as a Receiver, a bonus gift awaits you when you become sensitive to coincidence and synchronicity. As you develop your skills of observation, you will find your sense of what is "real" will expand. The world will become more *wonder*-full. It will come alive around you. You will experience nature, relationships, and life itself, differently. Everything you encounter will become more dynamic and more interactive. Your life will be enriched beyond measure.

TEST PROBABILITY

"What are the odds?"

This is a question that became part of my daily life for many months after Shera passed. Considering "probability" became a reflex I used with every "coincidence" I have described in this book. I would make an automatic assessment of the likelihood of it having happened randomly—by chance. *It was this essential reality check which helped give significance to what happened*, and encouraged the idea that somebody or something could have caused it to happen.

Assessing probability is a skill that is key to confirming a "sign."

This can become a powerful tool for you as a Receiver, as you reflect on occasions when you have noticed possible signs and messages. Often what had convinced me of a communication in the first place was how improbable it could be happening by chance—if at all. As the odds or probability of something happening "by accident"—by chance—became smaller and smaller, the validity of believing some other force or element caused them to happen increased. At times, even as I was watching an event unfold, it had already passed the probability test.

For example, in my account of drawing the two Joy cards from the word bowl with 800 cards, I already discussed the odds that make it virtually "impossible" these three cards could have been drawn in the way they were, merely by chance. (Chapter 5: Word Play)

Considering probability is a practical way to identify "evidence" that your loved one may be trying to communicate with you. It can also highlight the creative lengths to which a departed loved one can go to create messages which would normally be considered impossible, and which only you would notice and understand.

TRUST YOUR GUT

I think when we don't know what to believe, we usually default to a parallel question: "What do we *think*?" This assumes using your mind—thinking—will give you the clarity you are looking for and can depend on. "Thinking," however, may not be as reliable a guide as we assume it to be. In recent years, a new consensus is overturning entirely what it means to "use your mind."

Resonance is the extrasensory perception
That you are attuned with or relating to something.

This relatively new idea goes far beyond the generally accepted view that we have a logical, rational "mind" in our left brain and an intuitive mind in our right brain. It proposes that your mind is "relational." This will not be a surprise you if you accept the analogy of the brain being akin to a rail yard dispatcher, tracking and relaying impulses it receives from the body. Thoughts and memories are among those incoming impulses that inform the mind. Indeed, the mind may actually have no formal location, and merely be the global interplay of information stored all over the body.

This idea was developed as a way of explaining how people receiving organs from other people can discover memories *that aren't theirs* but those of the donors of the organs they received. There are documented cases in which transplanted organs even led to changes in personality. In one study fifteen percent of heart transplant recipients reported personality changes, and an additional six percent reported a "drastic change" in personality. In yet another report, for example, after receiving the heart of a biker, a previously mild-mannered, middle-aged woman became an aggressive, heavy drinker. In another report a man in his late fifties suddenly developed an uncharacteristic attraction to classical music for the first time in his life. He had received the heart of a young man who had been a passionate classical musician.

With this information, phrases like "muscle memory" and "cell memory" take on new currency. In addition, neurons, cells typically found in the brain, have been discovered in the heart, giving rise to use of the term "the heart brain." "Listen to your heart" may indeed be wise advice.

"Resonance" is the extrasensory perception that something is attuned with you or related to you. Its companion is emotion. So, I've learned when I don't know what to *think* about something, I check in with my gut heart—for what I "feel" about it. That is where I'll find the *resonance* I'm looking for that could identify a possible contact.

"Thinking about" or using logic simply does not compare to the power of resonance and emotion when it comes to being able to relate to events, link them together, weld them into a belief system, make memories permanent, and "lock" them into the body.

"Listen to your heart" may indeed be wise advice.

This all happened for me in the instant the poster appeared in my hands when I returned home from the crematorium. (Chapter 5: A Letter from Heaven) At that time, it was probable that the mental gymnastics, wondering, and hoping Shera might still be around could have continued in me for weeks or months. Instead, all of it vanished in an instant because I had an immediate *visceral* response. The resonance was clear in the spontaneous wave of emotion that washed over me in that moment, and I *knew* Shera was near. With such resonance I required no further thought for validation. Suddenly grief was out of place. A new certainty had replaced it. Shera *was* concerned for me, hearing me, looking after me, loving me . . . and communicating with me.

NOTE SIGNIFICANCE

Because signs and messages are intended for you, they will *always* have something of substance that relates either to the departed loved one, or to you, what you are doing, have done, or are considering doing. This could be a direct reference, or it could be symbolic. However, *it will always be something you can recognize.*

Whether or not you are dealing with a possible contact from the other side depends on whether it carries *meaning* of some kind for you—*significance.* For example the word which kept appearing after Shera left: "Joy." It had significance because it was the emotion we associated with her and her work. It was a word she often used *and* the brand we chose for her gallery.

> **Signs intended for you will always be something you can recognize.**

There are several things which can endow an event with meaning:

◆ Context. What happened before, during, or afterward? Who was present at the time?

◆ Coincidence. What made its timing perfect? How did it coincide with a person, an action, a revelation? a significant day, hour, or anniversary?

◆ Thoughts and Feelings. What intuitive thoughts, feelings or reactions are associated with the event?

Simply *wondering* whether something you have just experienced may be a sign or message could signal that—consciously or unconsciously—you have just recognized some of these signs. Any of them can indicate a communication has come your way.

You may become aware of this immediately or as you reflect on it sometime later.

Nevertheless, the challenge, as always, is that you may be the only one for whom an event or object may carry significance, or who even sees it at all. Thankfully, as I have already said, the doubt I expected to experience from others was largely a figment of my own imagination. They are usually interested and often respond with a story of their own.

Nevertheless it is important to accept with confidence the significance you recognize in an event, independent of whatever others might say or think.

◆ ◆ ◆

THE TAKEAWAYS

❖ A sign or message needs only to make sense to the person it is intended for.

❖ Often something in a message defies the odds of having happened at all.

❖ Resonance or gut feeling can be more reliable than thinking "logically."

❖ "Coincidence" and synchronicity are part of every sign or message from the other side.

The Fifth Lens—Really?

Belief is the basis of all our experiences. It is the foundation upon which we build our perception of reality. Our beliefs shape the way in which we engage with the world.

The possibility that we may be able to connect and even communicate with a loved one who is no longer in a living body lies outside the belief system of many people. That alone usually eliminates any likelihood of there being a connection, even if connection were something that is desired.

This fifth lens focusses on what creates and maintains our beliefs, so we can begin to look more consciously at the beliefs we hold. It reveals ways in which we can work with and begin to open "closed" beliefs so they can begin to allow the possibility that there can be life after death, and communication with departed Spirits.

Belief can be a Trickster. On one hand, your ability to see signs and messages from the other side can be blocked by *unconscious* beliefs and expectations that you are holding. Paradoxically, at the same time, beliefs you have *consciously* adopted can lead you to imagine "signs" and "messages" that are *not* there.

Believing something is *not* possible is a limiting belief, and it is always subject to change, because with one breakthrough, what once was thought to be not possible becomes possible in our minds after all.

Beliefs evolve as awareness grows.

Having the flexibility to shift your beliefs can expand your world.

CHAPTER 13

Changing Beliefs

A little child was walking hand in hand with her mother. As she looked at other people on the sidewalk around them, she became alarmed. She looked up at her mother, "Mommy, why is everyone bumping into each other?"

Confused, her mother looked around. "What are you talking about? There's nobody bumping into anyone!" And then she added, "Don't be silly!"

As a result, the little girl learned not to register what she was seeing.

◆   ◆   ◆

That little girl was Barbara Brennan. She grew up to become a meteorologist with NASA. After years working in the Goddard Space Flight Centre, the ability she had a child returned. She began seeing again the auras she had seen as a child. Once she was an adult, she was able to validate and embrace this ability as a gift. For the rest of her life, she dedicated herself to studying energy phenomena associated with the human body, and founded the Barbara Brennan School of Healing to further her work.

In her remarkable books *Hands of Light* and *Healing Hands*, she lets others see what she sees, through artist's renderings of what is revealed to her through her remarkable gift. The illustrations depict how the auras of people change when they are angry or worried, ill, or on drugs. It shows in their auras. These pictures effectively make something real—and believable—to people who are unable to see auras themselves.

◆　　◆　　◆

However, in our day-to-day lives, at some level, even people lacking Barbara's ability to *see,* can pick up on mood changes in others around them. How is that possible? It is because moods are a manifestation of emotion—they are an *energy.*

We do not have to be uniquely gifted or "chosen" to experience contact.

Each of us has this potential within us. Simply by shifting our intention and focus, we can become more conscious of the energy and emotions in the people around us. This makes it possible, once we tune in, to interact with them in a more effective way.

Similarly, as remarkable as my story with Shera may seem, the sort of things I was able to experience did not require me to be uniquely gifted or "chosen." *Such sensitivity is within the reach of anyone prepared to examine their beliefs.*

EXPECTATIONS

Having a belief automatically leads us to have certain expectations. Both beliefs and the expectations they give rise to can help you receive messages from the other side, *and* they can also blind you from seeing what is right in front of you. This can happen consciously or unconsciously.

In a remarkable study, subjects were asked to watch a short video after which there would be a question. They were told they would see two teams of three people each. These people would be intermingling randomly, all while throwing a ball back and forth to others on their team.

A couple of minutes later, when the video was over, the subjects were asked the question: "Did you see the gorilla?"

In the video, as the two teams were moving around each other, a man in a gorilla costume walked slowly across the room behind them—*in full view. Yet a third of the subjects failed to see him!*

❖　❖　❖

As children we were unable to test what we were told, and generally accepted it all without question.

Believing what they were told, they were *expecting* a question related to the activity they were told to focus on. As a result, they were blind to something that was happening right in front of them.

❖　❖　❖

Whether or not we will be able to recognize signs and messages coming from someone who has passed will depend largely on the beliefs and expectations we have. If we hold the belief such a thing as a message from Spirit cannot be "real," we make it unlikely we will experience one—even if we want to. That is what happened to Barbara Brennan when her mother told her what she was seeing was not real. She adopted her mother's belief and simply stopped registering consciously what she had been able to see.

It is a worthwhile exercise to become more conscious of the beliefs we hold. We will then be more able to see how we might be limiting ourselves.

When we arrived as newborns in this physical world, we learned spontaneously to recognize and respond to the physical phenomena we encountered. As we grew older, we learned how to *understand* them: what is "real," and whether it is dangerous or safe. These are things we learn from parents and friends. Because as children we were unable to test what we were told, we generally accepted it all without question. We *assumed* what we were told was true.

Grief is an initiation to a brand new world in which what is lost is not gone.

Although someone who has lost a loved one may be unaware of it, they are standing on the threshold of a new world, a world of spirit and subtle energies.

Whether one chooses to move into this new world or not is often determined by what they have heard from parents and friends about death and souls, and about life after death.

I believe that is why many people who may *want* to have connection with a departed loved one do not experience it themselves. They cannot imagine such a thing ever happening. Matt is an example of such a person. He believed he had lost his beloved Christa forever. (Chapter 9: Open to Receive).

Unfortunately, many go through life without considering such concepts as life after death, the evolution of souls, and reincarnation. As a result, when they are facing death themselves, or the imminent death of someone they love, they lack the conceptual resources that could have helped them manage the confusion and disorientation they have to deal with. Instead, they find themselves overwhelmed by their emotions and unanswered questions.

CHANGING BELIEFS

As a young man, when I thought about death, I assumed what I thought others believed, was true. It was simple: people died. They were buried. They went to heaven. Maybe there were ghosts. I did not consider the possibility of life after death. I had not heard of reincarnation.

To be honest though, it was not that I actually *believed* any of it, I just had assumed a position consistent *with what I thought others believed* and adopted it as *my* "belief." A sort of believing-by-association. I had never put any energy into determining if any of this was actually true or not, and therefore worthy of my belief.

> *I didn't decide what I was going to believe,*
> *I just assumed what I thought others believed was true.*

However, when I left the echo chamber of school classrooms and lecture halls, I began to encounter people with different opinions and at times radically different ways of seeing the world. Much of it was strange and intriguing; eccentric ideas that were hard to test. Things like life after death, regressions, talking to the dead, and reincarnation. It was hard to know what to believe . . . or even if any of it could be true.

Rather than decide all these people were wrong, or alternatively *assume* their opinions and beliefs were true, I was happy simply to keep all the possibilities alive. This mindset has been a godsend. It made it possible to learn things I never imagined about the world around me, particularly things beyond the physical realm.

MY SHELF

At some point in my younger life, in a moment of rare humility, I realized that how much I might "believe" something to be true, has absolutely no bearing on whether it actually is true or not.

About that time, I became aware that I had subconsciously created a place to "store" contrary, novel, and unproven concepts and theories. I picture it as an imaginary "shelf." For no particular reason, I think of it as being located above my left shoulder.

This system had one particular advantage: instead of letting my beliefs override unfamiliar ideas by default—slamming the door, so to speak, on possible opportunities—I could simply leave the concept on my shelf. I didn't have to determine its veracity.

Whatever I may believe, has no bearing on whether it's true.

The best part was that this shelf maintains and updates itself automatically. When I receive further information or perspectives related to any of these concepts, they get added, without my putting a great deal of energy into it.

Ultimately, if the original idea is validated again and again, through my reading, viewing documentaries, or listening to conversations, at some point it automatically "drops" off the shelf and into my belief system.

In this way I came to believe in the possibility of life after death. The accounts I had read and documentaries I'd seen had such consistency, one account after another, I now hold a conscious belief that death is not the end it is generally considered to be.

That was how this imaginary shelf helps me deal conceptually with the kind of intangible phenomena I have been describing here. I don't really have to "decide." I am free to be curious.

My belief system has evolved and expanded in response to newly discovered insights and these remarkable life experiences.

However because my sense of the world is subject to change, it is necessary on occasion, for me to do reality checks. My life has become a stimulating and ongoing lesson in discernment.

This has led me to identify three commonly held illusions.

ILLUSION 1: THERE IS AN ABSOLUTE REALITY

Humans tend to believe what they *need* to believe in order to feel safe. I once asked someone to explain how a controversial government bill which was about to be become law could protect us. She said, "I *have* to believe it will protect us, because I *need* to feel safe."

When things are stable and functioning, most people don't want to change anything. That is why the idea of being able to define what is absolutely true and real in our world is so attractive. However, this is an illusion.

We tend to believe whatever we need to in order to feel safe.

Beyond Our Senses

Humans tend to define the world in terms of what is observable, measurable, predictable, and enduring, as it is revealed to us through our sight, hearing, smell, touch, and taste. "If I cannot see it, touch it, or hear it then it does not exist."

Yet countless animals, dogs, bats, sharks, elephants, dolphins, and raptors for example, are all variously able to smell, hear, taste, smell or see a world which humans are totally unaware of. So how then could humans possibly define a "true and real" world which extends beyond what they can even detect?

The Limits of Science

It is true that science, through the proxies of various meters and detectors, has enabled humans to become aware some things exist which their bodies could not otherwise detect. However, it is unable to prove or define the existence of premonitions, intuition, or hunches as "real" even though almost everyone has experienced them. Together with clairvoyance and clairaudience, both long proven to be genuine phenomena in our world, this demonstrates that science too, is unable to define or explain reality in absolute terms.

ILLUSION 2: COINCIDENCES HAVE NO SIGNIFICANCE

In this "Age of Science," when someone hears a conclusion they do not agree with, it's not uncommon for them dismiss it.

"That's just a coincidence. I follow the science."

"Coincidence" is a word we use to defend our current beliefs.

The irony in this statement is remarkable! *That there was a coincidence is the point!* It could be said science is the study of coincidences.

Traditionally, when scientists notice things coinciding in time and space without any apparent reason, they initiate an experiment to arrive at an explanation of what that connection might be, and test it to see if they could create the same result.

Coincidence is a part of everyone's lives. Sensitivity to coincidence is a skill that helps reveal the dynamics of energy in both the non-physical world and spiritual realm.

ILLUSION 3: "DEAD IS GONE"

Humans are quite a complex phenomenon. We live in physical bodies which must be fed, watered, and protected. Yet we are also an energy body which cannot be detected by our physical senses.

At some point I realized Shera's vitality, her humour, her creativity, her joy, her personality—all the intangibles that comprised who she *was* and what I loved about her—*weren't physical.*

When Shera's physical body stopped, I accepted that the body—which had always "*been*" Shera—was indeed dead and here beside me. Therefore because her vital Soul essence and all that comprised her in life was no longer in evidence beside me, it was easy to consider it it too was "*dead . . . and gone*"

Yet while the dead body remained beside me, where was the "dead" spirit ? I suspect for millennia people have asked the same question.

Over the centuries many cultures, such as that of the Inuit woman mentioned have believed there is a vital essence which is embodied while the person is alive, which leaves the body at the time of death. This vital essence, this energy, or spirit, does not die but continues on.

"It has always been this way" is not always the best way to proceed.

◆　◆　◆

I believe these three illusions or assumptions tend to lock people into a mindset that does not easily allow them to develop a contact they might otherwise be hoping for with a deceased loved one. As people come to recognize their beliefs for what they are, they will be better able to choose whether they want to keep them in their belief system. Dropping or changing them would alter what they will *expect*—and subsequently *experience*—after a loved one passes. That means a person who started with the assumption that connection with someone who has passed was not possible, may discover that connection is becoming more possible after all.

PREPARING FOR CONTACT

There are several things you can do to facilitate the process of shifting your beliefs to something that will increase the odds of your having and developing the meaningful connections you may be looking for.

KNOW WHAT YOU BELIEVE

If you are unaware of what you believe, or have not developed your own personal beliefs, it is likely that you will be holding some views other people hold, without ever really having considered them critically.

The first step in preparing for connection, is to become conscious of what you believe.

Unconscious forces, forgotten memories, and emotional triggers can sabotage a relationship. In the same way your unconscious assumptions can sabotage your ability to recognize and work with the energies and events that will come up after someone you love passes on—*and these may be the signs and messages you are wanting to receive.*

"It has always been this way" may be a guide, but it is not always the best way to proceed. Simply being aware of this, though, makes other things possible. It will help you reassess what you currently believe. This awareness makes a new choice possible.

STAY OPEN

Once you are aware of what you currently believe, it becomes possible, with intention, to consciously evolve it. Instead of saying, "I don't believe that," for example, when you encounter new ideas that run against what you currently believe, you can say instead:

"I don't know."

"Maybe."

"Who can say?"

"Perhaps it is possible."

Once you have made space for new ideas, allow yourself to explore them. If topics come up about life after death and contacts from the other side, don't close the book, change the channel, or walk away from the conversation. After all, such is the way we are given gifts. It may not be all that long before you realize your belief has shifted. With that, new things become possible.

This work need not wait until someone has passed.

By creating the space to consider ideas that would otherwise fall outside of what you currently believe, you will start to draw concepts to yourself which better represent what is true for *you*. I was surprised to discover how much information suddenly began to appear once I did that—videos, stories, people, and accounts. Much of it was surprising information I had not seen before. All of it was validating the idea that ongoing connection is possible after death.

It is important to note that this work need not wait until someone has passed. Indeed, starting before there is any hint of death on the horizon means you are already prepared when the time comes.

RECOGNIZE BELIEF CLUSTERS

The change can come suddenly and very quickly. Often, when one accepts a new belief, it leads them quite naturally to acquire associated beliefs. For example, once you believe Souls don't die, you do not have to stretch much further to believe:

◆ There is a Soul independent of the body.
◆ There is life after death.
◆ People who have passed over can see us and care about how we are doing.
◆ It is possible to continue in relationship with someone after death.

Once you have allowed an idea you did not believe at all, to become "possible," the rest unfolds automatically.

For example, when Shera passed, the idea of an independent Soul surviving death, (the first two points above) was already part of the cluster of beliefs I held around death. So, it was not a big effort at all for me to believe that loved ones who have departed continue to care about us (third point above). Then, when the messages started coming, I had no hesitation in believing connection with a deceased loved one was possible . . . and it instantly joined my cluster of beliefs (fourth point above). It was not long before I had also added the belief that it is possible to continue in relationship.

We can only benefit by being aware of our beliefs,
and holding them softly.

TAKE SMALL STEPS

If you would like to have connection but cannot quite believe it is possible, it may help if you were to approach the question in two steps. First, in your head, change "This is not possible" to "I really don't know." This naturally awakens curiosity and ignites a desire to know more. It's a natural reflex.

Second, allow this curiosity to lead you into testing the idea by reading books and viewing documentaries and talking with others. A single video, a conversation with a survivor, or an unexpected event could flip things for you in an instant. (Chapter 5: A Letter from Heaven).

◆　　◆　　◆

Even if death is not something you are dealing with at the moment, there is value in consciously reviewing your current beliefs about death and afterlife and being open to other views. There are so many new ideas and unfamiliar things that lie beyond the world encompassed by our belief systems; we can only benefit by being aware of our beliefs and holding them softly.

Then, by the time death is on the doorstep, a belief once held that death is the "end" may have evolved into believing it to be a transition. With that change, the person you might once have believed was "lost" may continue as a dynamic and loving presence in your life—and the grief you might have felt would have become much more bearable, or fall away as it did with me.

❖   ◆   ◆

THE TAKEAWAYS

❖ There is no absolute or true "reality." Reality is a matter of perception.

❖ Beliefs can evolve and do not have to be permanent.

❖ With a little curiosity and an open mind, long-held beliefs that no longer serve you can be shifted in an instant.

❖ In the universal quantum field of energy, the energy body may be more "real" than the physical body.

❖ Beliefs come in clusters. A change in one belief is often associated with immediate changes in other related beliefs.

Whether we are aware of it or not, we create our reality moment by moment in the choices we make and the responses we have to every encounter, every situation, every emotion that arises or is triggered.

This is particularly true at times when a loved one passes on. Once we can become conscious this is true any given moment, and particularly at times when a loved one passes on, we have an opportunity to enrich our lives in ways we could not imagine before, transforming obstacles, challenges, pain—and even grief—into experiences that teach us, strengthen us, and nurture us, body and Soul.

This is what can add the gift of self-empowerment to the experience of loss.

CHAPTER 14

Starting Fresh

I am the master of my fate:
I am the captain of my Soul.

William Ernest Henley

What have I learned with my partner's passing?

For me, there's no doubt Shera is with me still. But there's so much more. In writing this book, my questions have taken me far beyond the remarkable connections I've had with her.

INSIGHTS

Because I had never thought much about "losing" someone—especially Shera!—or about grief, I have been amazed to find myself now writing thoughts I've never had before—flashes of insight that have taken me totally by surprise. It is as though they have been delivered to my mind by the momentum of this book unfolding at my fingertips. In a sense, this manuscript has become my teacher. Now, death and grief are no longer strangers to be ignored or avoided at all costs.

The greatest lesson I've learned in my quest, is that although death and grief may arrive in the guise of the Grim Reaper, to my surprise—behind the fear, the shock, and the pain of their arrival—I have discovered they are also working as a Divine Alchemist.

I now believe alchemy—transformation—is their *purpose*. For example, what was once embodied becomes a Soul; existing relationships can be healed or transformed; and as we glimpse the Mystery of life and death, the blinders that have covered our eyes vanish. Whenever this ultimate transition arrives, as it inevitably must, we are given an opportunity to transform our lives by accepting that there is a Bigger Plan, and a divine Order of Things.

> *Although death and grief may arrive in the guise of the*
> *Grim Reaper, they are also working as a Divine Alchemist.*

It is in the failure to address—*and accept*—our own impermanence in the face of the inevitability of death, that we, ourselves, become largely responsible for whatever fear we carry, and much of the shock and the pain we suffer when death ultimately enters our lives.

I see now why "understanding" our minds . . . discovering and consciously developing the beliefs we hold . . . can play such a key role in finding peace of mind.

In learning to become Receivers, we become a bigger version of ourselves. The different lenses of perception and belief described in this book are pathways to become more conscious, more aware. By developing our sensitivity to connect with a deceased loved one, we are also empowering ourselves to see beyond horizons we have always accepted. The sensitivity that allows us to recognize a message or a sign will transform us over time.

We have an opportunity to discover a world communicating with subtle messages of its own, offering gifts we could not imagine. Once acquired, this sensitivity is not limited to detecting signs coming from a departed loved one. It also has the power to break through the habits of our perception and let us encounter the wealth of stimulus, information, and synchronicities that swirl around us every day.

WHAT NEXT?

I have arrived at a new place. I think it's where my Soul, my inner Self, always intended I should be. Shera could always see that in me and has always wanted me to develop the confidence to own my power and stand in my own light.

I imagine wherever she is, Shera is celebrating as I, her "dear unfinished task," move ever closer to "completion." At one point, I said to a friend, "Who I Truly *Am* is finally replacing How I Have Been in my life." *In that instant* an eagle flew directly into my line of sight beyond the tips of my fingers, its white head ablaze in the golden light of the evening sun!

Learning to continue loving, to love beyond grief, sets us on the threshold to merge with an infinite world.

As I reflect on it, perhaps now my beloved Shera, satisfied that her work here is done, may move on to other projects. If that is to be the case, I feel no sadness in it.

I have accepted that over time, the connections that I've had with her, and so relished, may not come as often or be as intimate. This may simply be her affirmation that I'm doing okay now, flying on my own.

We will forever be connected, and I know from time to time there will always be occasional sweet synchronicities and reminders.

How do I know? Because, like all who have suffered loss of a loved one, I've learned that I carry that power in my own heart.

❖　　❖　　❖

AFTERWORD

A Call To Action

This is a powerful time in human history.
Momentous changes are taking place in our world—
and they are not limited to the physical realm.

◆　　◆　　◆

There is a reason we, as a human species, are interdependent. Since the
beginning of time, storytelling has been the prime force in expanding the
knowledge and insight of communities around the world. Our collective
wisdom as humans has grown through the conversations and insights we
have shared about the things we have experienced.

What one person shares can spark a fire in the minds of others.

Imagine if people felt free to speak more openly of contact they have had
after the passing of a loved one, and shared the insights they have gained;
and if we were all more curious and open to hearing their stories.

OUR STORIES CHANGE THE WORLD

We need to have these conversations. We need to talk with one another
more often—with our family, and friends—sharing our experience

around death and grief so others can benefit from what we've learned and where we've found comfort. What we share could also be a long-needed antidote to the apprehension and dread felt now by so many whenever they think about the inescapable departure that awaits them and those they love. Sharing our experiences can spark insights for all of us, illuminating the Mystery death evokes, and revealing the gifts that come with it.

Our stories, when shared, would validate similar experiences others have had and wondered about. They would make it possible even for others who have not yet been in this place, to recognize and to understand it in ways most people have missed for countless generations: Love goes beyond grief. Relationship with the one who has gone ahead can continue.

◆　　◆　　◆

As more of us tell our stories, and more people come to expect contact with their departed loved ones, the "other side" will seem less far away. In this emerging Age of Higher Consciousness, such awareness will lead us to more direct—and perhaps even interactive—connection with those who have gone ahead.

◆　　◆　　◆

Acknowledgments

I am profoundly grateful for the support I have received from so many sides in the writing of this book. These three years have taught me much about humility and generosity and transformed my sense of who I am and what I am capable of.

Thanks to Shawn, Marilyn, and Ollie right at the outset, for so willingly listening as my fledgling stories and ideas began to take shape in our conversations, and for encouraging me to develop them.

Thanks to friends Nisha, Lorill, Eroca, Raven, Michelle, Nick, and Yvon who held the vision of this completed book without question despite the times I was stuck and struggling. Their confidence in the outcome was invaluable in getting me to the finish line.

I have been blessed as well to have had countless generous souls, short term volunteer workers, whose work here has freed me to further my writing, and whose interest and willingness to listen to my stories encouraged me along the way.

I am grateful to the first readers: Laura, Vickie, Kathleen, Gary, Jon, Gayle, Jennifer, Debra, Anna, Julie, Robert, Austin, and Lainey. Their feedback helped me to assess the impact of the book and helped in my finding solutions to aspects of the book that needed to be restructured.

The contribution of my editors, Kirsten and Valerie led to invaluable changes and improvements in the manuscript.

And of course thanks to Steve, Cristina, Geoffrey and the remarkable team at Steve Harrison's Bradley Communication, who provided coaching, expert guidance, and invaluable resources for me in the process of learning that a manuscript is only a fraction of what goes into creating a book, publishing it, and making it successful.

I give thanks daily to God and whatever muse and angels have contributed to the evolving context and structure of the book, for their support—and the insights that I share in this book. I feel blessed—and surprised—to be the channel through which these ideas are making their way out in service to the world.

And of course while mentioning angels, I have eternal gratitude to my special Angel, Shera, who has quite literally "overseen" the whole project. She has played such a central role in moving her "dear unfinished task" further toward completion . . . a completion that I suspect, will continue unfolding as I move ahead.

I look forward to what comes next!

◆   ◆   ◆

About the Author

CHIDAKASH JORDAN

Chidakash enjoys awakening curiosity in people and encouraging them to view their lives as an adventure. As a young man driven by an ever-present desire to discover new places and perspectives, he left his native Canada, and travelled extensively in Europe, North Africa, South Asia, Peru, and Australia.

While in Australia, he was appointed National Education Officer for a United Nations affiliated organization, and established the *"ideas centre,"* an educational initiative, to bring Third World voices and viewpoints into schools across the country.

Upon his return to Canada, he met Shera, his life partner. Together they built Serenity by the Sea, a fairytale-like cedar "castle" retreat centre on Galiano Island island in the west of Canada. For twenty-six years, in a program called *The Next Step*, they worked with people facing life changes, helping them empower themselves to start moving forward again in their lives.

They also led people to Machu Picchu in a spiritual journey they called *Enter the Mystery*. Over eighteen years they guided their travellers along the Inca Trail and into the mysteries of the fabled world of the Incas, simultaneously encouraging them to explore the new discoveries and awareness of themselves that the experience was awakening within them.

Chidakash has always been motivated to help people move with their passion and find their unique voice, identify the gift they carry within them, and share it with a world waiting to receive it.

After the years of caring for Shera before she left, Chidakash was profoundly transformed by the extraordinary contacts he has had with her, and the life-transforming succession of events he experienced after her passing.

Living now on Salt Spring Island, he dedicates his time to letting who are experiencing the pain of losing a loved one, know how they can create a different and gentler experience for themselves, in which their loving relationship can continue beyond death.

Chidakash Jordan is available for speaking engagements and media interviews. You can also visit *ChidakashJordan.com* to sign up to receive resources and complimentary materials to go deeper into this topic.

He can be contacted at *peace@ChidakashJordan.com*.

◆　◆　◆

The Next Step

Dance On! Love Beyond Grief is the first of three books in a trilogy called *Soul's Dance—The Alchemy of Grief.* The following two books are to be published in 2024 and 2025:

◆ *Master the Dance—Grief as Alchemist and Midwife*

◆ *Dancing to a New Tune—5 Steps to Transform Grief*

◆   ◆   ◆

VISIT MY WEBSITE: peace@ChidakashJordan.com

Sign up for my Newsletter for tips on managing the challenges of loss.

◆ Receive more in-depth articles.

◆ Discover stimulating insights and new perspectives.

◆ Find new options and personal resources to empower you.

◆ Read examples of breakthroughs and transformation.

◆ Get updates and excerpts from my next books.

FOLLOW ME ON FACEBOOK

◆ Check out the stimulating quotes, and memes.

◆ Share your insights and your stories. I welcome guest posts.

I WOULD LIKE TO HEAR FROM YOU

Please send me an email at peace@ChidakashJordan.com if you would like a one-on-one conversation exploring questions and issues you may be dealing with around loss.

MEET WITH ME

I invite you to contact me:

- ◆ to speak to your group in person or online
- ◆ to join you in a podcast or media conversation
- ◆ to join you in a zoom call
- ◆ to address a public gathering
- ◆ to do live readings and workshops

HELP GET THIS MESSAGE OUT TO THOSE IT CAN HELP

- ◆ Gift this book to a friend who is navigating the loss of a loved one.
- ◆ Recommend it to people you know who are dealing with death and grieving.
- ◆ Bring it to the attention of professionals who support people dealing with loss: Hospice Centres, Care Homes, Senior's centres, Grief counsellors, End of Life Doulas, Funeral homes, Libraries, Hospitals and Death Cafés.

SHARE YOUR STORY

If you have experienced connection or ongoing relationship with someone who has passed, please contact me.

- ◆ Have you felt you were still connected to a loved one after they passed on?
- ◆ What happened to create that sense of connection?
- ◆ How has that impacted your life?

◆ Have you got a message to help others after loss or who are dealing with loss?

These stories need to be shared more widely so that we can give more and more people a new expectation of what is possible after a death.

Your story could join other stories in a compilation that will comfort people feeling the pain of grief and empower them with options that can help them transcend grief and transform their sense of loss. Reach out to me at peace@ChidakashJordan.com.

◆   ◆   ◆

Manufactured by Amazon.ca
Bolton, ON

38465086R00150